WAINWRIGHT
ON THE
LAKELAND MOUNTAIN PASSES

Also by A. Wainwright and Derry Brabbs

FELLWALKING WITH WAINWRIGHT
WAINWRIGHT ON THE PENNINE WAY
WAINWRIGHT'S COAST TO COAST WALK
WAINWRIGHT IN SCOTLAND

WAINWRIGHT

ON THE

LAKELAND MOUNTAIN PASSES

with photographs by
DERRY BRABBS

GUILD PUBLISHING LONDON

This edition published 1989 by
Guild Publishing by arrangement
with Michael Joseph Ltd

Typeset in 10½ on 13pt Linotron Ehrhardt
by Cambrian Typesetters, Frimley, Surrey

Colour reproduction by Anglia Graphics, Bedford
Printed and bound in The Netherlands by
Royal Smeets Offset b.v., Weert

CN 3342

CONTENTS

MAPS BY BORIS WELTMAN
Illustration on half-title page: *High Sweden Bridge*
title page: *Honister Pass*
page 4: *Hallin Fell from the pier at Howtown*

INTRODUCTION

T HE LAKE DISTRICT is a compact mass of high and rugged ground soaring abruptly from surrounding valleys and the coastal plain of Cumbria, almost as distinctive and well defined as a volcanic island rising from the sea. Within its natural boundaries, mountains and fells crowd together, there being over 200 separate and named summits. As in all mountainous terrain, the peaks are linked by ridges intersected by skyline gaps or depressions that permit ease of crossing from one valley to another; a few carry roads but most are accessible only on foot. These relatively simple ways of crossing high ranges are known as passes. Long before men explored the lofty summits for pleasure, the passes were used by nomadic tribes and later by the early settlers and, where negotiable by packhorses, by enterprising traders as commercial routes.

Left *Helvellyn from High Tove*   Above *The road over Honister Pass*

Lakeland is not fashioned for motorists: cars can penetrate the interior only in a few places. It is largely a preserve of walkers. The most exhilarating and rewarding form of pedestrian travel is fellwalking, a pastime that has grown greatly in popularity in recent decades, but it is available only to the physically fit. Most visitors to the district, however, are content to stroll along the lovely valleys and beside the lakes, preferring not to risk the hazards of the higher ground above; some even have a primeval fear of mountains as places of danger. But there is an intermediate class of walkers who admire mountain scenery and favour the loneliness of the wild recesses, yet because of disability or lack of energy in their later years cannot aspire to the ultimate summits and dare not venture too far upwards. Such are catered for by the passes, away from the sight and sound of traffic, where the peaks can be viewed in intimate detail and in the silence of solitude.

Deepdale

For those who can walk in moderation and choose to do so sedately and without fear of going astray, the passes offer ideal expeditions. People get lost on the mountains but very rarely on the passes. Here distinct paths have formed through centuries of use although they are often still narrow and rough; cairns provide comfort in places of doubt; the natural configuration of the ground, rising on both sides, confines walkers to the trodden ways, and the streams descending from the passes are infallible guides to direction. All these reassuring factors make the passes practicable in any weather conditions except deep snow, and on days when heavy cloud rules the tops out of bounds the passes can be walked in safety.

The passes may of course be walked in either direction. In this book, I have described them in the direction most usually followed or which provides the greater interest or excellence in forward views. In a few cases where passes have no official name, I have given them appropriate ones.

Every skyline gap or depression on a mountain ridge, sometimes referred to as cols, may be regarded as a pass of sorts if approachable on both sides, and there are hundreds of such places in Lakeland. Most of those remote from tourist paths will have been crossed by shepherds or foxhunters or Ordnance surveyors at one time or another, but many are virgin and have never been trodden by man. These latter are outside the scope of this book which is concerned only with those that carry distinct paths and are in common use.

Some of the passes are short and can be reversed to the starting point in the course of a day's walk. But most are of several miles and a single crossing is enough for one day. Walkers who are travelling from one bed-and-breakfast to another in a different valley have no problems, but those encumbered by cars must plan to return to them. The best arrangement in such cases is to team up with friends who also have their own transport, the two parties leaving their cars at either extremity of the pass at agreed parking places and doing the walk in opposite directions, swapping car keys as they meet midway, thus ensuring a comfortable return to base.

No day in the Lake District needs be wasted because of inclement weather. The mountains are inhospitable in bad conditions and better avoided, and touring the gift shops in the valleys and sheltering in doorways and cafés quickly palls. The friendly passes offer the perfect answer. You'll still get wet, of course, and despair at the shroud of mist that masks the beauty all around, but the exercise will do you good and after a rousing supper in dry clothes you will vote the day a very satisfactory one after all. Walking the passes is the next best thing to walking on the mountains and often no less rewarding.

Each pass is the subject of a separate chapter, the description of the route being accompanied by a simple location map with a mile-scale, north being at the top. Heights are given in English feet and distances in English miles despite the current regrettable practice of quoting them in foreign metres and kilometres to which the author, a jingoistic Englishman, refuses to comply. This book is about the English Lake District. Let's go on thinking of it as English!

1 BLACK SAIL PASS, 1800'
Wasdale Head – Ennerdale

WASDALE HEAD, the most impressive inhabited place in Lakeland, is so deeply inurned amongst high mountains that there appears to be no easy escape from it other than by reversing the usual line of approach on the road alongside Wastwater. Only the glen of Lingmell Beck coming down on the right below the shapely pyramid of Great Gable seems to offer a possible way out of the valley: this is the walkers' way to Sty Head. Less obvious is a route entering the side valley of Mosedale on the left: this climbs to a skyline depression or saddle between Kirk Fell and Pillar and descends from there into Ennerdale.

This is the Black Sail Pass.

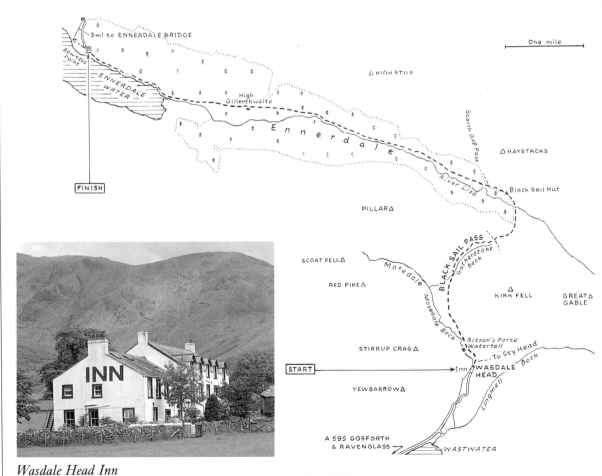

Wasdale Head Inn
Opposite *The top of the Black Sail Pass looking to Kirk Fell*

11

Wasdale Head

THE ROUTE STARTS from Wasdale Head Inn which has reverted to its former name after being known as Wastwater Hotel for many years, inappropriately because the lake is a mile distant. Modernisation has destroyed the old atmosphere of this venerable inn, a Mecca for the pioneers of rockclimbing of a hundred years ago.

When I first went there, the passages were littered with climbing ropes, hobnailed boots and drying clothes. Meals were served at a long table, with no choice of food, in a room hung with enlarged photographs by Ashley Abraham, whose camera work incidentally has never been bettered, of the classic rock climbs around Wasdale and the brave men who made the first ascents. The talk then was exclusively of adventures on the crags. Mine host in those early years of the sport was Will Ritson, a great character and practical joker: it was said of Wasdale Head in those days that it had the highest mountain, the deepest lake and the biggest liar in the country, the latter distinction being earned by Ritson himself.

Those times are over. Today all is changed. The inn has been tidied, the horses and traps have been replaced by cars, and sandals are as likely to be seen as heavy boots. I liked it better as it was.

A short lane leaves the inn heading towards Kirk Fell which most closely overlooks the dale, and a good path turns left above the intake walls and enters Mosedale. Just below, lined by trees, is Mosedale Beck, momentarily excited by a waterfall known as Ritson's Force; across the stream rise the towering slopes of Yewbarrow, surmounted by the cliffs of Stirrup Crag. Ahead, the desolate hollow of Mosedale comes into view, dominated by the ramparts of Red Pike and terminated by Scoat Fell.

The path trends to the right as the slopes of Kirk Fell decline. It climbs steadily to come alongside the tumbling waters of Gatherstone Beck, its name apparently derived from the boulders that litter its bed. This is forded, the path rising on the far bank in zigzags before straightening into a steady climb

towards the depression ahead. A newer track branching to the left is used by walkers ascending Pillar. Views here on Gatherstone Head are restricted to Yewbarrow behind and Kirk Fell across the beck, but gradually the gradient eases and a ruined wire fence marking the top of Black Sail Pass is reached.

Mosedale　　　　　　　　　　　　　　　　　Above *Ritson's Force*

At the top of the pass a splendid view unfolds ahead. Ennerdale is below in a dark shroud of conifer plantations contrasting sharply with the bare slopes of the upper reaches of the valley. Haystacks is directly in front and the lofty High Stile ridge rises in fine array to the left. At this point, however, the most arresting sight is Kirk Fell nearby, its shattered and craggy slopes soaring into the sky with dramatic effect: it looks rough, and it is.

The fence crosses the top of the pass, keeping to the watershed; westwards it serves as a perfect guide to Pillar, eastwards it climbs sharply into the fastnesses of Kirk Fell, bravely accompanied by a thin track.

The path goes forward and descends into Ennerdale, coming alongside the edge of the plantations and crossing the River Liza by a footbridge. Now in sight are the two giants of Ennerdale, Great Gable and Pillar: the former descends in smooth slopes from the rim of crags fringing its perfect dome while Pillar is very rough from top to toe and has an unbecoming skirt of spruce fir.

Black Sail Hut is a few minutes further on.

Opposite *Black Sail Hut*   Above left *View of Pillar from Ennerdale and* (right) *the River Liza*

The Black Sail Hut, once a shepherd's bothy but now converted and extended into a Youth Hostel, is a lonely outpost indeed, far from other habitations, but a first-class centre for fellwalking expeditions. A cart track, now used as a forest road, leads down the valley through the plantations, some relief from a monotonous trudge being afforded by the lively Liza alongside. Another Youth Hostel at High Gillerthwaite is passed after an hour's walk in the close company of trees, the forest road continuing to run alongside the north shore of Ennerdale Water, where there is a fine retrospective view of Pillar, to a public car park at Bowness Point. If no car is waiting, the walk can be continued by a lakeside path to the little community of Ennerdale Bridge to sample the fleshpots on offer there, these consisting of an inn, a shop and an infrequent bus to Whitehaven.

2 BOARDALE HAUSE, 1200′
Patterdale – Boardale or Martindale

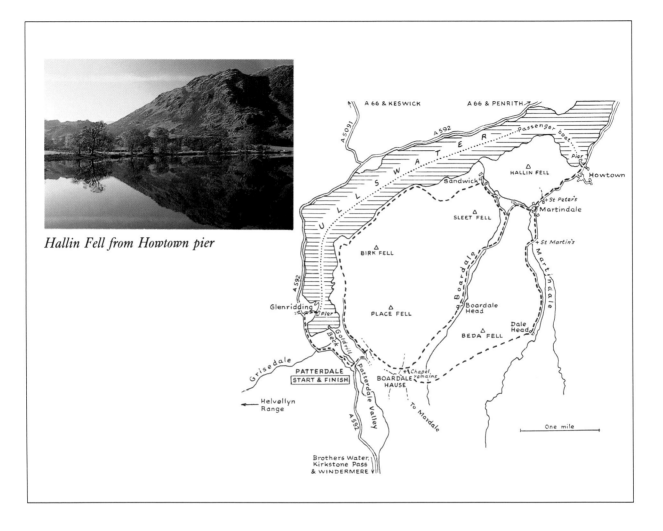

Hallin Fell from Howtown pier

THE EASTERN SIDE of the upper reaches of Ullswater rises abruptly in the steep and rough slopes of Place Fell, effectively barring a direct approach to the valleys that lie in the folds of the hills beyond. These valleys are hidden from the sight of the crowds of tourists who visit the lake, are unsuspected and remain unspoilt. By road, they can be reached by a long and circuitous journey around the north end of the lake and, having no through routes, are of little appeal to motorists, but walkers are blessed with a choice of two lovely paths. One runs along the lakeside, rounding the north end of Place Fell, and is in my opinion the most beautiful walk in Lakeland; the other climbs to and crosses a low ridge at the south end.

This latter pass is Boardale Hause.

Opposite *Patterdale from Boardale Hause*

Deepdale from Boardale Hause

FROM PATTERDALE VILLAGE, a side road crosses Goldrill Beck and gives access to the open fellside. The well-trodden path to the right is followed, taking the higher branch when it forks and climbing steadily to the easier ground of Boardale Hause.

The views on this ascent are of superlative beauty. Ahead is Brothers Water and Kirkstone Pass, deep-set amongst encroaching heights; behind is a glorious prospect of the Patterdale valley with the massive bulk of the Helvellyn range towering beyond the deep trench of Grisedale. Ullswater completes a delightful picture.

Boardale Hause is a walkers' crossroads, five paths leaving here for different destinations and needing care in selection. On the hause is a ruined enclosure resembling a derelict sheepfold, but in fact it is the site of a medieval chapel, as a few carved stones lying around testify. On large-scale maps, this is named Chapel in the Hause. Its isolated situation on the ridge, midway between Patterdale and Boardale, was presumably intended to give equal facility of access to the good folk of both valleys. Some years ago, the confusion of paths was further compounded by the construction of an aqueduct across the hause when the pipe-laying operations and tractors carved new routes over the top, but nature is doing its best to remove the scars.

Boardale Hause is the popular springboard for the ascent of Place Fell and a track climbs to the left with the summit as objective; another goes right for the long upland crossing to Mardale, but the main path, for Boardale and Martindale, leads forward over the crest, forking at once for Boardale, to the left, and Martindale, to the right.

The path into Boardale (spelt Boredale by early writers and map-makers) descends to the head of this valley which takes the form of a narrow defile between the slopes of Place Fell and Beda Fell. A good track goes down to the first habitation, Boardale Head, where it matures into a narrow road which, after a further mile or so, branches left to Sandwick; here the lakeside path may be taken to return to Patterdale, thus completing the circuit of Place Fell. The right fork links with Martindale and goes on to Howtown.

The path to Martindale is in no hurry to descend and circles around the head of Boardale to the south ridge of Beda Fell, beyond which it declines steadily into the much larger valley of Martindale, where there is a long-established deer sanctuary. It reaches the first habitation at Dale Head, a farmhouse notable for its massively buttressed walls. Here starts a pleasant road that proceeds along this quiet and lovely valley in the shadow of Beda Fell and joins the road from Boardale. Before the junction, a detour to the old church of St Martin is recommended: this was built in 1653 on the site of an ancient chapel, but was closed in 1881 because of decay. A new church, St Peter's, was built in 1882, but a few summer services are still held in the old church which has been restored.

Boardale

Dale Head

Below *The old church of St Martin*

From the road opposite St Peter's church a wide grass path – a joy to tread even in bare feet – leads to the top of Hallin Fell, and if time permits a half-hour's diversion, this simple stroll should not be missed. This is the easiest of all fellwalks and the visual rewards more than recompense the slight effort needed. Martindale is seen full length and in all its glory, and a bird's-eye view of Ullswater presents itself when the highest point is reached at 1271′. The summit is crowned by a fine obelisk of cut stone twelve feet tall. The man who built it not only indicated the top of the fell but erected for himself a permanent memorial.

There is a rise in the road beyond St Peter's church and at the top Ullswater is revealed ahead. The lakeside hamlet of Howtown is also in view amongst trees at the foot of a long descent made easier for cars by a series of wide loops.

Martindale from Hallin Fell

Howtown has a pier and is a calling place for the passenger boats that ply on Ullswater in summer. With pre-knowledge of the timetable, arrival can be timed to meet the boat for Glenridding, a mile from Patterdale, which gives a very pleasant return to the starting point of the walk. There is no more beautiful scene in the district than the head of Ullswater and no better way to enjoy its delights than to approach leisurely over the water.

Opposite *The road curling down to Ullswater*   Below *The pier at Howtown*

3 THE BURNMOOR CORPSE ROAD, 900′
Wasdale Head – Eskdale

BEFORE THE EARLY settlers at Wasdale Head were granted the present small patch of consecrated ground their fatal casualties had to be conveyed for burial elsewhere, at first to the mother church at St Bees and later to the churchyard just outside the village of Boot in Eskdale. The route adopted for these sad journeys to Boot lay over the low moor around Burnmoor Tarn, this being preferred to the longer and circuitous way on the primitive roads of that time. The coffins were strapped to the backs of horses, wheels being unable to negotiate the rough ground. The route was known as the Corpse Road and, now classed as a bridleway, is in popular use by today's walkers.

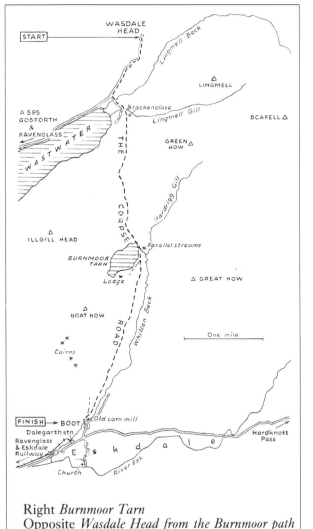

Right *Burnmoor Tarn*
Opposite *Wasdale Head from the Burnmoor path*

TURN OFF the road from Wasdale Head near the head of Wastwater where a lane to the left crosses an area that still bears traces of a devastating cloudburst in Lingmell Gill many years ago when an avalanche of boulders and rubble thundered down on the fields below, the debris being later partially cleared by prisoners of war. Beyond is the handsome building of Brackenclose, headquarters of the Fell and Rock Climbing Club since 1937. From here the route heads south on a gradual incline between the rising slopes of Green How and Illgill Head, to reach the bare summit of the pass, where Burnmoor Tarn and the fells around Eskdale come into view. The path goes on to the tarn.

Burnmoor Tarn is a large and unattractive sheet of water in a desolate landscape; a former gamekeeper's lodge is the only habitation in sight. The path skirts the eastern shore and here an odd natural curiosity will be seen: the main feeder of the tarn, Hardrigg Gill coming off Scafell, and the issuing stream, Whillan Beck, occur side by side and only a few paces apart without any apparent watershed between them.

After a marshy tract the path commences a long straight descent to Boot in the close company of Whillan Beck with the scene ahead becoming more pleasant with every step.

Walkers with archaeological interests and time to spare should deviate by climbing the low moor on the right to its summit, Boat How, thence descending south through an area of Bronze Age occupation with at least five stone circles and many ancient cairns as evidence. At the foot of the slope a bridleway will be reached, this going down to join the main path as it enters Boot.

Illgill Head   *Ruins near Boat How*

On the outskirts of Boot, before going down to the main street, the fellside immediately south is of nostalgic interest, being scarred with the remains of disused iron mines that were served by a narrow-gauge industrial railway along the base of the fell. The track is plain to see, although robbed of its lines, as is the site of the former Boot Station, passengers also being carried on the railway. This section was closed when the mines were abandoned, but half a mile down the valley the railway is open for passenger traffic; miniature trains offer a sylvan ride from Ravenglass to a new terminus at Dalegarth, where there is a shop and café. This popular railway is the Ravenglass and Eskdale Railway, affectionately known as Ratty, and links with the main railway at Ravenglass.

The old railway track at Boot

The village of Boot is entered by crossing a bridge over Whillan Beck and here is a building of character: the old corn mill, long disused but restored to working order by Cumbria County Council in 1975.

The scenery upstream is charming and a short walk on a woodland path from the bridge brings into view a delightful section of the beck, its waters tumbling in cataracts amongst rocks.

Boot is the 'capital' of mid-Eskdale although having only a few cottages and a tiny population. It is a friendly place and apart from its visual delights, has an hotel, shops and cafés that cater mainly for the summer invasions of visitors brought by the miniature railway to the terminus nearby. And there is a church and graveyard worth visiting, and of course the lovely River Esk. Boot is favoured.

The corn mill at Boot   *Whillan Beck*

4 CARLSIDE COL, 2250'
Millbeck – Barkbeth

ANYONE TRAVELLING between the Vale of Keswick and the countryside west of Skiddaw will almost certainly make the journey by road and only the odd eccentric with time to kill will consider the alternative walking route described in this chapter, this involving a steep and stony scramble in terrain unfamiliar to tourists. The route provides an introduction to the twin valleys of Southerndale and Barkbethdale coming down from Skiddaw, rarely visited and known intimately only by the local farmers. Other walkers are not likely to be met. Solitude reigns.

THE WALK STARTS at the pleasant hamlet of Millbeck nestling amongst trees at the base of Skiddaw where a path leads north and soon comes alongside the stream issuing from the obvious defile ahead. Directly in front is the dark pyramid of Carsleddam, a heathery offshoot of the greater fell of Carl Side beyond. The stream, Slades Beck, comes round the obstacle on the east side, down a stony ravine with Skiddaw Little Man towering high above and the parent fell ahead. The walk by the stream is so totally enclosed that it becomes claustrophobic: there is little of beauty in this arid scene. When confronted by the great mass of Skiddaw the route trends left and climbs steeply and stonily to an obvious col on the skyline where a deserved halt may be taken and the way onward prospected. Carl Side rises on the left, terminating a ridge formed by Long Side and Ullock Pike. A track bound for Skiddaw crosses the col and ascends a stony slope littered with slate fragments, some loose, some in embedded upright flakes. Nearby is the insignificant Carlside Tarn.

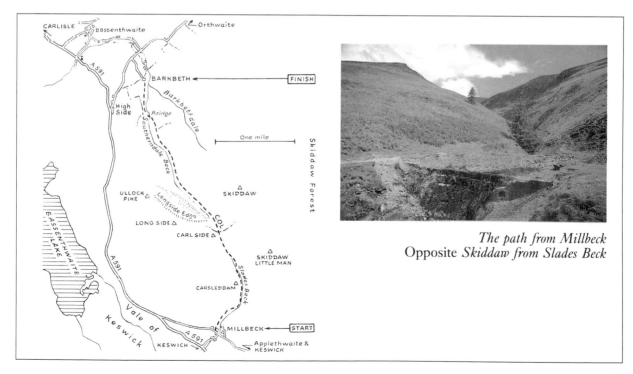

The path from Millbeck
Opposite *Skiddaw from Slades Beck*

Above *Long Side and Ullock Pike from Carlside Col*
Left *Southerndale*

Over the crest of the col the way is downhill on
steep pathless slopes into the head of Southerndale,
a shy valley completely dominated by the ramparts
of Longside Edge high above, from which fans of
scree scar the fellsides. When Southerndale Beck
takes shape, a thin track above its eastern bank will,
if it can be found, ease the walk down the valley to a
bridge, and here there is an impressive retrospect of
the valley with Skiddaw now in view.

From the bridge, a rough lane, with thorn bushes
and trees which soften the landscape, leads to the
farmstead of Barkbeth at the foot of a parallel valley,
Barkbethdale, along which is an imposing view of
Skiddaw.

A farm access lane goes down to a tarmac road
leading left to High Side, which has a bus stop on
the Keswick–Carlisle service. Or alternatively, a
side road goes to the nearby village of Bassenthwaite
(locally called Bass) which is likely to have refreshments on offer.

Above *The path to Barkbeth*

Below *Barkbeth Farm*

5 COLEDALE HAUSE, 2000'
Braithwaite – Lanthwaite

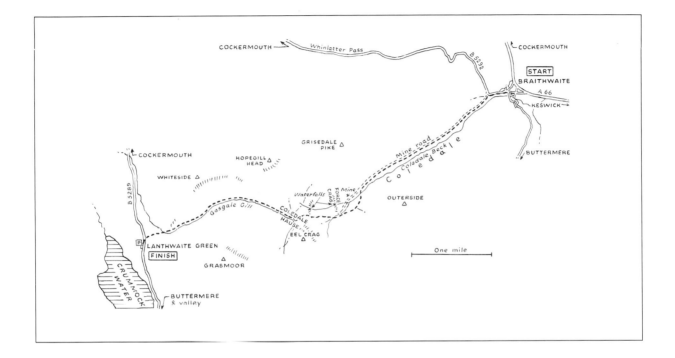

THE NORTH-WESTERN fells form a compact mass, the individual summits being closely linked, and although the boundaries of the group are clearly defined by surrounding valleys, there are no easy ways through the high ground.

The only recognised pass in common use is Coledale Hause, the usual route to it being along the straight channel of Coledale, leading into the heart of wild uplands, an approach also popular as a fast way to the summits of the enclosing heights, especially when starting from the village of Braithwaite. The through route is interesting rather than impressive, views being restricted, but the journey is a splendid half-day's expedition.

Opposite *Coledale*
Right *Braithwaite*

STARTING FROM Braithwaite, advantage can be taken of a long and easy mine road leading straight as an arrow in the direction of the hause. The village is left by the Whinlatter Pass road and around the first corner the mine road leaves on the left. There is a short cut to it blazed by the boots of the thousands of walkers bound for Grisedale Pike which dominates the scene, but the original start is much easier. The mine road enters the long valley of Coledale and heads purposefully for a barytes mine at its terminus: this section is tedious but gives a fast approach on a good surface along the base of Grisedale Pike; opposite is the shapely peak of Outerside rising sharply from Coledale Beck alongside the road. When the mine is within easy reach, the beck is crossed and a rising path ascends grassy slopes to outflank the imposing barrier of Force Crag directly behind the mine and forming a precipitous background. The dark cliffs are relieved by the silver thread of Low Force cascading over the rim.

As height is gained along the path, another wall of crags comes into view above the other, these upper cliffs also having a slender waterfall, High Force.

Force Crag

Coledale and Force Crag mine from High Force

Now having the impending mass of Eel Crag on the left, the path continues to climb easily to the flat expanse of Coledale Hause, passing many industrial relics on the adjacent ground. On the hause itself is a disused water cut that formerly diverted the stream of Gasgale Gill, coming down on the left, from its natural course over the watershed to provide supplies for the mines.

Most walkers arriving at the hause leave the path here to ascend Eel Crag or Grasmoor on the left, or Hopegill Head or Grisedale Pike on the right; all these fine summits are often visited in a circular expedition from Braithwaite using the hause only as a crossing place.

The through route to Lanthwaite and Crummock Water goes forward over the watershed and descends steeply into the ravine of Gasgale Gill on a path now much rougher underfoot but compensated by the lovely vistas appearing through the portals of the gill as the walk proceeds.

All around is wild desolation, ahead is enchantment.

As height is lost, the confining fells rise starkly into the sky. On the left is Grasmoor, the highest of the group, its steep slopes not inviting ascent; and on the right, even more repelling, are the crags and scree runs of Whiteside in an awesome downfall.

Between the two heights, the stream and the path run close together and emerge in a rocky passage at the exit to the gill; immediately a beautiful prospect is revealed as an easy slope goes down to the road at Lanthwaite Green. The formidable slopes of Grasmoor fall away abruptly to permit a view of the Buttermere valley with the High Stile ridge supreme. Over the pastures of Lanthwaite, rise the twin summits of Mellbreak, a stretch of Crummock Water also being seen.

The whole scene is exquisite and becomes more so on close acquaintance; only the procession of cars along the road disturb the tranquillity of this loveliest part of Lakeland. The road remains narrow despite the influx of summer motorists who must continue to suffer inconvenience: it would be sacrilege to widen and improve this road to modern standards, so destroying the charm of a delightful journey in scenery of superlative beauty.

Mellbreak and Lanthwaite   Above *Gasgale Gill*

Above *High Stile and Crummock Water*

Below *Crummock Water and Loweswater*

6 DALEHEAD TARN, 1900'
Newlands – Honister Pass

THE HEAD OF Newlands is so tightly encircled by mountains that there seems at first sight to be no way of crossing this barrier except by serious climbing. And these mountains are formidable. Blocking the direct route south is Dale Head, defended by cliffs always in shadow and effectively terminating the valley. Nor are its near neighbours of kinder appearance: high on the left is the mile-long escarpment of Eel Crags, a place for rockclimbers only, and to the right rise interminable slopes, capped by cliffs and scree, to the top of Hindscarth, neither having anything to offer the average walker.

Newlands Beck points the way of escape. It is seen coming down easier ground to the left of Dale Head and a path follows its course upwards without difficulty and leads on to an easy descent to the road at the top of Honister Pass.

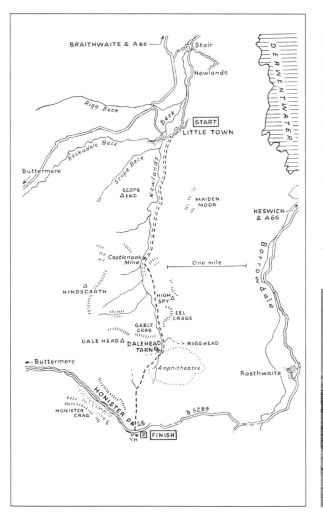

A CART-TRACK leaves the road at Little Town in Newlands and heads south following Newlands Beck upstream for two miles along the floor of the valley with little gain in height. The track is distinct, having been used for centuries by traffic from the many mines hereabouts, all now disused, and in modern times by the boots of walkers. On the left is Maiden Moor, with relics of lead mines and quarries, and on the right Scope End rises abruptly in a dark covering of heather that conceals the spoil of the once-famous Goldscope Mine; although the levels driven into the fellside can still be found, they should not be entered.

Opposite *The upper Newlands valley*
Below *Dale Head*

Hindscarth and Stile End from Little Town

This mine was abandoned over a hundred years ago after intermittent operation for six centuries: one of the oldest mines in the district, it was also the most important in output, having rich veins of lead and copper, and silver and gold have also been extracted. Its early development on a large scale was undertaken by German miners, and its long history has been marked by many incidents and much litigation.

Higher in the valley the old mine of Castlenook occupies a prominent headland alongside the track and beyond is revealed the final reaches in the form of a grassy ampitheatre deep-set amongst rising fellsides. Directly in front, leaving nobody in doubt that Newlands has come to an end, towers the immense facade of Dale Head with Gable Crag conspicuous. On the left skyline is the intimidating array of Eel Crags, and Hindscarth on the right is capped by a barrier of broken cliffs and has no welcome to offer. The ampitheatre, however, is a rewarding place for those with an interest in things past: there are mine shafts and ruined huts, and it is still possible to trace a well-graded path going up to the old copper mine on Dale Head, now in sad decay but worthy of inspection.

Newlands Beck is seen coming down from a depression to the left of Dale Head and a path follows it up to a plateau of easy but undulating and confusing ground. A track branches left to Rigg Head and descends to Rosthwaite past the extensive disused quarries.

For Honister, the path goes forward, still alongside the stream, passing Dalehead Tarn which cannot be seen but is indicated by a tributary issuing from it. A thin track leaves the side of the tarn bound for the summit of Dale Head which towers behind.

It will now be appreciated by walkers that the name of Dalehead Tarn heading this chapter is not really appropriate. The true pass or watershed is seen half a mile further on above a slight slope, the stream still descending from it. The path continues easily, crossing an old wire fence to join the main path from Honister Pass to the top of Dale Head. At the watershed, a glorious panorama of well-loved mountains is suddenly displayed ahead with stunning effect across the trench of Honister, and makes a magnificent background as the path descends gradually to the road at the top of Honister Pass.

Right *Dalehead Tarn*
Below *The view south from the watershed*

7 DEEPDALE HAUSE, 2150'
Dunmail Raise – Deepdale

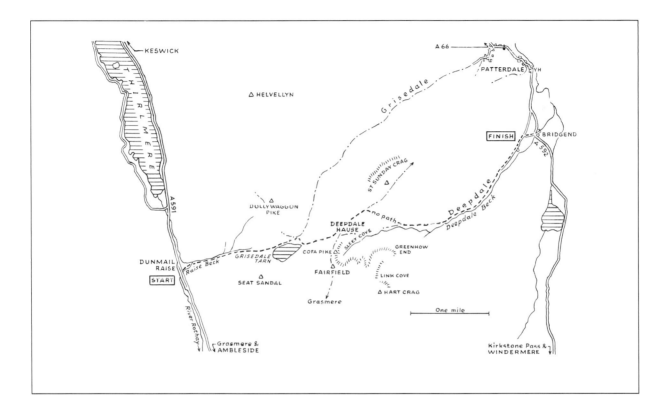

WHEN I FIRST explored the eastern fells, there was no semblance of a path from Grisedale Tarn to the obvious depression of Deepdale Hause on the high skyline between St Sunday Crag and Fairfield. Since those early days, a thin track has formed, not, however, intended to assist the crossing of the hause into the valley of Deepdale beyond but to reach the excellent path going up from the hause to St Sunday Crag after following the ridge down from Fairfield. Rarely indeed is the hause used as a pass into Deepdale since most walkers arriving at the tarn from Grasmere prefer the easier route provided by continuing along the bridleway down Grisedale and so to the Patterdale valley, of which Deepdale is a part. But if Grisedale is busy with pedestrian traffic, as it often is, Deepdale Hause is the key to a lonely alternative with mountain scenery of a high order, and for the person who likes undisturbed solitude it has special appeal for there is very little possibility of meeting other walkers. Here a buzzard may circle overhead and sheep will be grazing but no other sign of life need be expected. On its wild upper reaches, Deepdale becomes your very own.

Opposite *Deepdale Hause from Grisedale Tarn*

GRISEDALE TARN is invariably reached by way of the popular Grasmere–Patterdale path but there is a shorter and quieter route to the tarn from the west. This starts from the A591 on the top of Dunmail Raise.

Clear of the tarmac and the things that speed along it, the moor is crossed to come alongside Raise Beck issuing from a rough watercourse forming the north boundary of Seat Sandal. The beck, a happy tumble of cataracts, is no longer destined exclusively for the Rothay, as nature intended, but has been diverted to feed Thirlmere. A stony track climbs along the bank emerging, as Seat Sandal declines, into open grassland with Grisedale Tarn in full view ahead, backed by the St Sunday Crag and Fairfield range with Deepdale Hause clearly identifiable. Nearby is the massive bulk of Dollywaggon Pike carrying a dusty path to Helvellyn.

From the outlet of the tarn, a beeline can be made for the hause, keeping a lookout for the new track to ease the ascent of the rough fellside. When attained, there is a comprehensive view of the Helvellyn range seen over the great gulf of Grisedale, but the most imposing feature within close proximity is the sharp pinnacle of Cofa Pike, concealing its parent fell, Fairfield.

The Helvellyn range from Deepdale Hause   Above *Raise Beck*

Used as a pass, a descent must now be made into the head of Deepdale without the help of a path, and the scenery is immediately awesome: the crags of Cofa Pike plunge precipitously into Sleet Cove and beyond is seen the massive wall of Fairfield in a succession of cliffs and scree gullies which terminate in the towering buttress of Greenhow End. There is no difficulty in finding a way down the valley: after initial steepness, the descent is on easy grass and Deepdale Beck soon forms to give infallible guidance – indeed, one has a feeling of watching a tremendous convulsion of nature from a comfortable seat in the front row of the stalls.

When the wild upper recesses are left behind, a path materialises and leads around the base of St Sunday Crag in surroundings of lessening drama to the cultivated fields, trees and scattered homesteads as the A592 road and creature comforts are reached in Patterdale.

Above *Cofa Pike*

Below *The northern precipices of Fairfield*

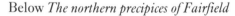

8 DUNMAIL RAISE, 782'
Grasmere – Thirlmere

THE MAIN ARTERY of communication in the Lake District is the A591 road which takes advantage of the only easy breach in the high fells. Recent road improvements have made this a fast highway for cars but, because of the weight of traffic, heavy lorries are precluded from using it.

The name of the pass derives from Dunmail, the last King of Cumberland, who was defeated in battle in 945 by King Edmund of England, and whose remains, according to legend, are buried beneath the huge pile of stones on the summit of the pass. This cairn or mound was preserved during a realignment of the road some years ago and now occupies an island formed by a dual carriageway.

Freed from the delays caused by heavy vehicles, cars use the road as a racetrack. Pedestrians are advised to keep off the tarmac as much as they can and may do so as described below.

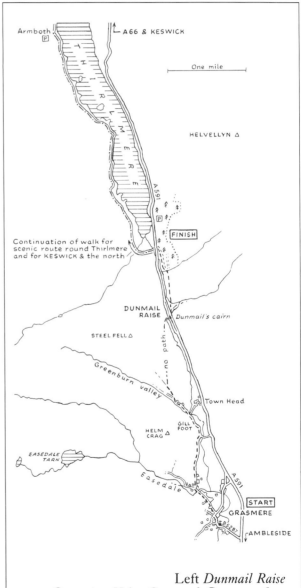

Left *Dunmail Raise*
Opposite *Helm Crag and Grasmere from Dunmail Raise*

INSTEAD OF following the A591 north from Grasmere, travellers on foot would do far better by taking the side road to Easedale, leaving it at the first junction on the right where a quiet and pleasant byway runs below Helm Crag to the secluded dell of Gill Foot and continues along a track that leads into the side valley of Greenburn. This is left near the last two cottages in favour of a path climbing the south ridge of Steel Fell. When clear of the intakes, which still feature a pillbox where the folk of Grasmere intended to repel German invaders who never came, a beeline can be made to Dunmail Raise, now clearly in sight, by contouring the pathless fellside and crossing an area of drumlins left by a glacier. Walkers arrive exactly at the top of the pass, indicated by Dunmail's cairn.

The alternative to continuing on the road is provided by a stile in the wall on the east side, which admits to a field where the old road can be joined to cross an ancient bridge at the foot of a series of waterfalls before entering a conifer plantation and debouching on the main road opposite the junction of the scenic route around Thirlmere. If instead the A591 is followed down to Thirlmere, a tear-jerking plaque set in the wall on the right, and not noticed by speeding motorists, deserves a brief halt: this pays a glowing tribute to a horse that gave his master a lifetime of faithful service and 'whose only fault was dying'.

Walkers bound for places north of Thirlmere, or Keswick, should escape from the A591 and take to the scenic route, a much quieter and more attractive alternative starting at the junction where a signpost still points to Armboth although nothing is left of Armboth now but its name which is used for the car park and the fell (*see* page 100).

9 ESK HAUSE, 2490′
Eskdale – Borrowdale

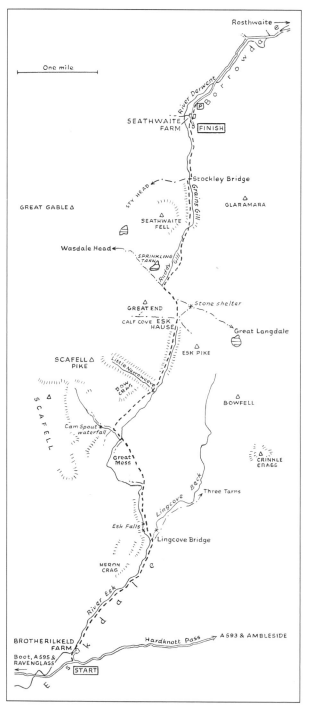

ESK HAUSE – the true Esk Hause, not the misnamed one – forms a watershed between the two lovely valleys of Eskdale and Borrowdale, and is the highest pass in Lakeland. This distinction is not recognised by popularity, for although it crosses magnificent terrain it is rarely used as a pass. In fact, I have never seen anybody engaged on the through route and, truth to tell, I have never done it myself. One reason for its neglect may be that the course of the route runs alongside the Scafell range and most red-blooded walkers, in fine weather, cannot resist the greater appeal of the high-level traverse of the ridge.

The head of Eskdale is confusing topographically, a tangle of rough ground in a bowl formed by the Scafells, Esk Pike, Bowfell and Crinkle Crags, and one of the wildest areas in the district. But the route to Esk Hause is clearly defined by the River Esk, this being followed closely to its source just below the hause and pointing the way exactly. Over the hause, territory much frequented by walkers is reached and the loneliness of the approach is dispelled.

But make no mistake. An afternoon start is too late. Esk Hause deserves a full day.

ESKDALE'S ROAD is left at the foot of Hardknott Pass near Brotherilkeld Farm, the only habitation seen on the journey until Seathwaite Farm is reached at the end of the day. A distinct path goes up the valley in typical Lakeland scenery and comes alongside the delightful River Esk, a watercourse of pools and splashes and happy gurgles, but today its charms must be resisted: it must not detain. The long precipice of Heron Crag, high on the left, is passed and a confluence of waters is reached, the picturesque stone arch of Lingcove Bridge being just beyond and spanning Lingcove Beck coming down from Bowfell.

Opposite Esk Hause

Above *Brotherilkeld looking towards Bowfell*

Below *Lingcove Bridge*

Hereabouts, the Esk changes direction, the river issuing from a spectacular gorge through which plunge the Esk Falls. The gorge is manifestly inaccessible and is avoided by crossing Lingcove Bridge to a path rising along the fellside high above. Almost at once the great wall of the Scafells comes into view ahead, a thrilling moment calculated to stop in his tracks anyone carrying a camera. The path goes forward towards the imposing scene and reaches a vast marshland, the Great Moss, once a deer preserve owned by Furness Abbey. Now the Scafells are seen in full stature and majesty, rising sharply from the flat strath of the Moss. A popular route of ascent is indicated by the waterfall of Cam Spout directly ahead, but the route to Esk Hause follows the river up the valley opening on the right and after gingerly picking a way through the marshy ground, join a firm path.

Above *Esk Falls*

The Scafells from Great Moss

The path continues upriver, the valley narrowing as the fells crowd in on both sides. The formidable cliff of Dow Crag, sometimes referred to as Esk Buttress, is prominent on the left and succeeded by the great chasm of Little Narrowcove, a rough and menacing ravine beset by crags and bringing a tributary down to join the Esk, which is now in its infancy. As it traverses stony ground the path becomes intermittent as it still keeps close to the stream. The eastern flanks of the valley throughout this section of the walk from Great Moss belong to Esk Pike.

The hause is now seen ahead above a rough steep slope; the stream and the path give up the ghost, having fulfilled their roles as guides, and a final stiff pull lands the walker on Esk Hause, with a new landscape in front of him.

Above *Esk Pike*

Below *Looking north from Esk Hause*

Grains Gill

On the grassy expanse of Esk Hause life becomes exciting again. The ground in front falls away gradually towards Borrowdale between the massive dome of Great End, half left, and Esk Pike high to the right. Well-worn paths are met here. A track blazed by thousands of boots each year winds up into Calf Cove on a popular route to Scafell Pike; another goes off to climb Esk Pike. Another, also part of the Scafell Pike route, comes up over easy grass from a wind shelter of stones on the path crossing below between Great Langdale and Wasdale Head; this shelter is commonly regarded as Esk Hause, quite wrongly.

To proceed, it was formerly necessary to go down to the shelter and turn along the Wasdale path, but a fairly new track has been trodden from the hause and descends directly to the Wasdale path at the top of Grains Gill after passing alongside Great End and revealing a view of Great Gable. Grains Gill is the key to the last few miles of the walk. At its head, alongside the Wasdale path, it has the name of Ruddy Gill, the red subsoil having an iron content. Five minutes further towards Wasdale, the path comes alongside the shores of a delightful sheet of water, Sprinkling Tarn, a great time-waster and not on today's crowded itinerary: it should be saved for a leisurely visit and a long halt. Having resisted this detour, the stream issuing from Ruddy Gill is crossed and a steep descent follows, skirting a deep ravine from which the stream emerges as Grains Gill. This too is forded to a path that goes down with the stream to Stockley Bridge; the stream becomes the River Derwent below the bridge. The crowds met here should not be assumed to be a welcoming party; nothing is further from their minds. Some are picnickers; some casual strollers. We are back in tourist country. A wide, dusty and often busy path leaves the bridge for the short journey to Seathwaite Farm, always a welcome sight. There is a car park here which is the terminus of the Borrowdale valley road.

Above *The top of Floutern Pass looking to Buttermere*

Below *Ennerdale from Floutern Pass*

10 FLOUTERN PASS, 1300'
Ennerdale – Buttermere

IF WALKERS WERE called upon to vote for the Lakeland pass they considered least attractive, there is little doubt that Floutern Pass would top the poll with a thumping majority. This pass is the easiest and shortest way of crossing the fells between the Buttermere valley and Ennerdale Water. It starts well and finishes well but the intermediate stages are without charm or beauty and contain an extensive quagmire from which few walkers escape dryshod. Nor have the surrounding fells any visual appeal: they are barren, lack character, are without features of interest, undistinguished in outline and share in the general hopelessness of the landscape. It is the sort of place that once visited will ever afterwards be approached with trepidation. Some reward for misery will be gained by walking the pass in the direction here indicated, suffering being forgotten in the sylvan beauty of Buttermere with Scale Force as a special bonus to revive drooping spirits. Floutern, frankly, is a mess.

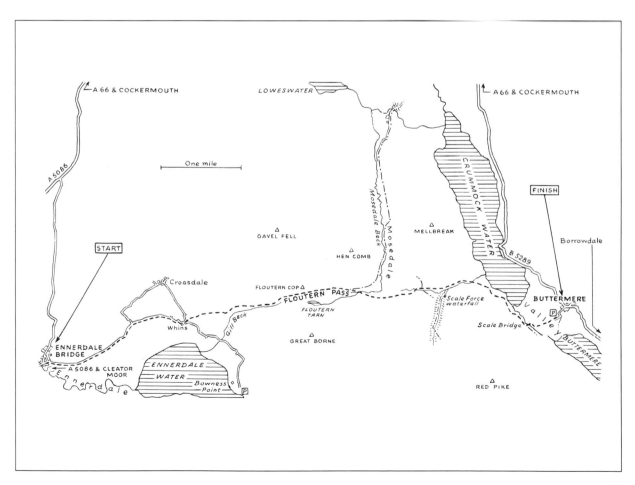

THE VILLAGE of Ennerdale Bridge is left by the Croasdale road, from which a lane cuts a corner to reach a no-through road, much used in summer, going down to a large car park at Bowness Point on the side of Ennerdale Water. The path to Floutern Pass leaves this road at Whins and climbs steadily alongside Gill Beck to a wire fence crossing the watershed and marking the highest point of the walk. The views fore and aft are in total contrast. Behind are the green pastures and thriving husbandry of Ennerdale with a glimpse of its lovely lake, a pleasing scene, but ahead is seen a dreary wasteland without invitation or welcome – Bunyan's Slough of Despond in person, but with a hint of better things in the far distance. Only the diminutive peak of Floutern Cop nearby tries to give distinction to the scene. On the right, the ground rises to Great Borne, also known as Herdhouse or Herdus, and Floutern Tarn comes into sight as the walk proceeds, being revealed as an elongated sheet of water with attractions only for anglers and not worth a visit.

The path descends into a vast hollow, dark with peaty marshland and threaded by the stream issuing from the tarn. The stream has the good sense to escape into a side valley, one of Lakeland's five Mosedales, and a path goes with it along the base of Mellbreak to the sweet countryside of Loweswater. But walkers bound for Buttermere must contemplate the morass ahead and find a way across it, gingerly treading the wet ground and making abortive searches for firm footing in a series of trials and errors before soaked feet make a nonsense of patient investigation and a beeline is ploughed to the greenery ahead. Finally clear of the glutinous mud, a slight slope is climbed and at the top a view is revealed that makes it all seem worthwhile.

The marshes of Floutern Pass

Crummock Water and the Buttermere Fells
Right *Scale Force*

After the damp rigours of the Floutern crossing, the prospect from the top of the rise beyond is a soothing balm. Crummock Water appears in a frame of colourful fells to make a lovely picture. On the descent, a popular path turns off to the rocky chasm of Scale Force, its 125-ft plunge making it the highest of Lakeland's waterfalls and the highlight of the Buttermere area. Victorian ladies and gentlemen visiting the force were brought by boat to a landing on the shore of Crummock Water, but today's Elizabethans must use a wet path through the lakeside trees. This is the path that ends the walk from Ennerdale, crossing Scale Bridge to enter Buttermere village in surroundings of such exquisite beauty that Floutern seems like a bad dream. But if the path is crowded and noisy, as is all too often the case, even lonely Floutern will be seen to have some merit after all.

11 GARBURN PASS, 1450'
Troutbeck – Kentmere

THERE IS little doubt that in late medieval times before the present lines of communication were established, a primitive road cut across the fells in the south-east corner of the Lake District between Windermere and Shap. The initial section of this ancient highway took advantage of a dip in the high skyline of the Ill Bell range to cross from Troutbeck to Kentmere, the depression being known as Garburn Pass, originally spelt Garbourn. Ordnance Survey maps still name the long lane leading to it as Garburn Road. Today, reduced in status to a bridleway, it is a route only for walkers, pony trekkers and motorbike scramblers.

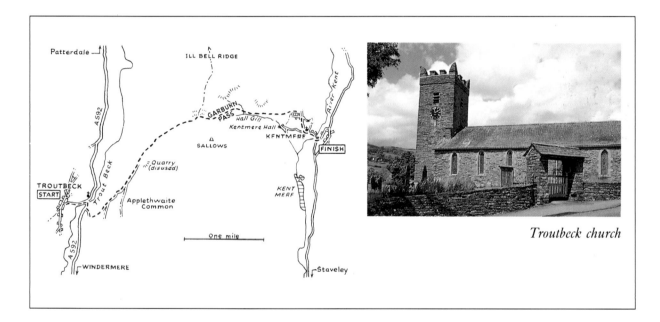

Troutbeck church

A SHADY LANE leaves the A592 near Troutbeck church and climbs steadily among trees to reach open country where it is joined by a rough road coming from the south. The fellside here is Applethwaite Common, the venue of annual sheepdog trials.

The lane continues to ascend between stone walls and soon reaches the disused Applethwaite Quarry. Most old quarries are gloomy and repelling, with an air of desolation, but this one, masked by trees, is worthy of inspection since it still retains its weighbridge and other relics of abandoned industry. This apart, there is little to relieve the tedium of the steady climb except for an excellent aerial view of the Troutbeck valley, improving with every step.

When the summit is gained, there is a comprehensive panorama to the west, the high fells of Lakeland forming the distant horizon. A rough track turns off here over marshy ground to the Ill Bell ridge, but the cart-track goes forward through a gate between sturdy stone walls.

Opposite *Ill Bell from the Garburn Road*

Above *Applethwaite Quarry*

Below *Garburn Pass looking down to Windermere*

With the Kentmere valley now in sight, the descent there commences on a deteriorating but distinct path following Hall Gill down below an escarpment of crags high on the left. In pleasant surroundings, the pele tower of Kentmere Hall comes into sight below and the new Kent Mere beyond. As the first buildings appear ahead, a huge isolated rock may be noticed in a field over the wall on the right: this is Badger Rock, also known as Brock Stone. It resembles a small cliff, large enough to provide rock climbs, but is in fact a boulder fallen from the heights above.

Pass through a picturesque complex of cottages and farm buildings to a tarmac road which leads to Kentmere church and the village beyond.

Pele tower at Kentmere Hall

Above *Badger Rock*

12 GATESCARTH PASS, 1950'
Longsleddale – Mardale

MOTORISTS TRAVELLING north from Kendal along the A6 are rewarded for preferring this old turnpike to the modern M6 by a brief glimpse of a lovely valley opening between bare fells on the left after five miles of the journey. This valley is seen emerging, straight as a furrow, from a distant mountain surround, and patterned by pasture and woodland and an occasional white farmhouse. With the River Sprint running alongside, it is a delightful place.

This is Longsleddale, the most easterly of the major valleys of Lakeland and lacking nothing of the beauty of the others; indeed, preserving the romantic charm that some have lost. Because of its seclusion and the absence of a through passage for vehicles, and having neither an inn nor a shop in its eight-mile length, it has happily suffered little from the intrusion of tourists: its one road remains narrow between fragrant hedges and stone walls. It is an oasis of pastoral tranquillity amidst inhospitable fells, looking very much as it did three centuries ago. Man has nurtured it, not spoilt it. The only disturbance to its rural security occurred some fifty years ago when Manchester Corporation cut a five-mile trench along the eastern slopes to contain their aqueduct from Haweswater, but they restored the ground commendably and nature has since clothed the scars. More recently a second aqueduct was planned but the project was abandoned after angry protests from the inhabitants. The people of Longsleddale may be few in number but they love their valley and are right to be proud of it. Longsleddale is delightful.

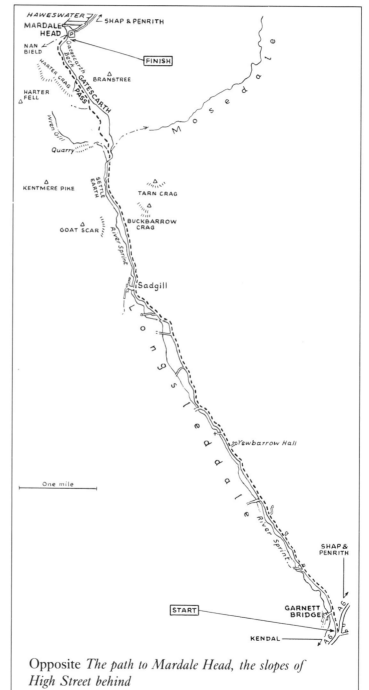

Opposite *The path to Mardale Head, the slopes of High Street behind*

Longsleddale
Right *Garnett Bridge*

THE VALLEY ROAD branches from the A6 and descends sharply to the only hamlet, Garnett Bridge, where a cluster of cottages around a former bobbin mill makes a picturesque study for the camera. Then the road goes on, mile after mile, passing the oldest building in the dale, the medieval pele tower of Yewbarrow Hall, and the little church before finally reaching the farmsteads of Sadgill. Here the road ends. Cars can go no further and are often parked on the verges by the bridge, sometimes awkwardly to the annoyance of the few residents of this lonely outpost. Car parks never improve the scenery and usually detract from it, but at Sadgill Bridge a small one is now needed.

At Sadgill, the view ahead is of wild grandeur. The mountains crowd in, revealing the desolate upper reaches of the valley through the rugged portals of Goat Scar and Buckbarrow. The crossing of Gatescarth Pass starts here, for travellers on foot only. The tarmac road gives place to a rough cart-track between stone walls. The green pastures continue for a further half-mile. In 1845, a reservoir was planned here with the authority of an Act of Parliament to regulate the flow of the river to the water-powered mills lower down the valley, but it was never proceeded with because of the huge cost. Cultivation ends abruptly where a gravel dam, built to retain the stones brought down by the river, crosses the valley floor.

Now the track starts to climb into a scene of grim desolation. On the left rises the precipitous face of Goat Scar, this being succeeded by the gloomy mountain hollow of Settle Earth, a haven for foxes; the summit above is Kentmere Pike. On the right towers Buckbarrow Crag, its discharge of stones littering the ground; amongst them but not discernible from the track is a massive boulder rivalling in size the famous Bowder Stone in Borrowdale. The height above is Tarn Crag which has on its summit the crumbling remains of a stone survey post, one of three erected above the line of the aqueduct from Haweswater, here in a tunnel over a thousand feet below the surface.

The steeper sections of the track are roughly paved with stones set in horizontal courses to serve as brakes for the horses bringing down heavy loads of slate from Wrengill Quarry, long disused. Alongside tumbles the infant Sprint in a series of cataracts and waterfalls.

The head of Longsleddale

The cart-track escapes from its confining walls when the gradient eases and a gate is reached, the wall on the right turning up the fellside and that on the left continuing on the line of march. The landscape here is dreary, the walk proceeding with open grassland on the right, rising gradually to a depression on the skyline. A path branches in this direction over rough and marshy ground: this is the way to Mosedale.

A stile in the accompanying wall admits to the vast disused Wrengill Quarry, and for walkers with an interest in industrial archaeology a detour over the wall will be most rewarding.

Wrengill Quarry has vertical man-made cliffs, tunnels, a derelict tramway, water channels, a terrace of cottages and ancillary buildings, all in sad decay.

On my first visit, the cottages were substantially intact. I once spent a night here amongst the skeletal ghosts of an abandoned industry, an eerie experience in the graveyard of dead workings. The only pleasure I can remember on this occasion was provided by the extensive carpet of wild thyme on the cliff tops: I uprooted a few plants for my garden at home but they obviously preferred the loneliness of Wrengill Quarry and soon withered in an alien habitat in suburbia.

At the far extremity of the quarry, Wren Gill enters in a fine waterfall, disappearing into two potholes and continuing underground before emerging as the River Sprint.

The quarry was last worked by Italian prisoners during the First World War. It is a sad place today.

Waterfall in River Sprint

Summit of Gatesgarth Pass
Right *Harter Crag*

Resuming the walk to Mardale, the track rises steadily over grass slopes, now unenclosed, and ascends in a series of zigzags, engineered centuries ago to ease the passage of laden packhorses. Higher, the gradient lessens and the summit of Gatescarth Pass is reached at a gate in a wire fence crossing the watershed. A new landscape opens up ahead framed by the crags of Harter Fell and the steep declivities of Branstree. The prospect is pleasing as the track descends into Mardale, at first gently and, when the ground steepens, in a succession of sharp zigzags so delightful to follow that there is no inducement to short cuts; consequently there is little erosion and the path remains in pristine condition. Gatescarth Beck is a lively companion alongside.

To the left, split by a great gully, tower the cliffs of Harter Crag. It was here that a pair of golden eagles, the first seen in Lakeland for 150 years, built an abortive eyrie two decades ago. Later they adopted a nesting site on another crag a mile away where, under the watchful eyes of wardens of the Royal Society for the Protection of Birds, they settled successfully and reared families.

High Street and Haweswater come into view during the descent and the path from Nan Bield joins in for the final hundred yards to the public car park at Mardale Head situated at the terminus of the road alongside Haweswater.

13 GOATS HAUSE, 2100'
Coniston – Duddon Valley

G OATS HAUSE, as the name implies, is undoubtedly a pass, and it is true that by crossing it a walker may travel between Coniston and the Duddon Valley, but few ever will because the Walna Scar 'road' is so obviously the most direct way from one to the other. Only for anyone wishing to extend the walk and having a couple of hours to spare can Goats Hause be recommended. The route, however, has one great merit: it passes through one of the grandest scenes in the district where the awesome precipices of Dow Crag soar high above Goats Water. Also introduced is Seathwaite Tarn, a large sheet of water shyly hidden in a fold of the hills and not often seen by Lakeland's visitors.

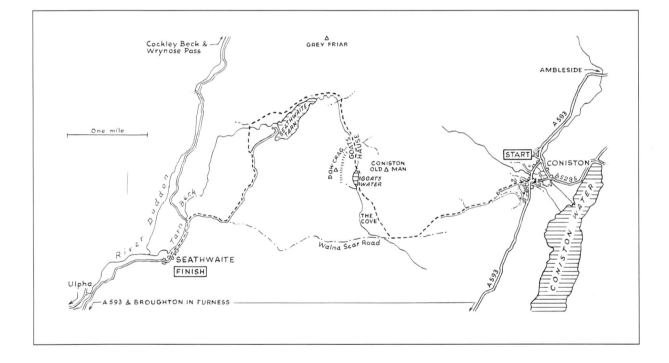

APPROACHING FROM Coniston, leave the Walna Scar cart-track just beyond the rock gateway where a track branches to the right and rises into a hollow, The Cove, with Dow Crag coming into sight ahead. When Goats Water is suddenly reached after a rise in the path, a dramatic picture unfolds with stunning effect. Dow Crag is now revealed in full stature as an array of massive buttresses split by deep gullies and overtopping steep slopes of scree and boulders falling to the water's edge. Goat's Water is uninviting, its outlet choked by boulders and its shores fringed with debris from above.

Opposite *Dow Crag*

When I first visited this impressive scene, there was an upright memorial stone, roughly inscribed CHARMER 1911, on a grassy bank amongst the boulders at the outlet of Goat's Water. Charmer was a foxhound killed in a fall on Dow Crag, and it is nice to reflect that a faithful dog was revered in this way. Then came the vandals. On a later visit, I found the memorial uprooted and cast among the stones in the bed of the issuing stream. Later still I could find no trace of it and hope it has been carried down by floodwaters to a safer haven. Charmer deserved better than this.

The rockclimbers' way to Dow Crag fords the outlet and slants upwards across the scree to a cave formed by a huge boulder at the foot of the cliff, this being the usual base of operations. Lesser mortals take a rough track along the eastern shore of the tarn, reaching easy slopes that rise to the dip in the skyline ahead. This is Goats Hause, traversed by a path linking Dow Crag and Coniston Old Man, the latter having been on the right throughout the walk thus far. There is a fresh landscape in front but it is the sight of Dow Crag that still rivets the attention.

Goats Water and Dow Crag from Goats Hause

Seathwaite Tarn
Right *Gully on Dow Crag*

Continuing, a long simple slope descends into the valley in front where Seathwaite Tarn, almost a mile in length, occupies the centre of the stage, the backcloth being formed by the bulky fell of Grey Friar, an outlier of the Coniston range. Around the head of the tarn, which has been adapted as a reservoir, are relics of the Seathwaite Copper Mines, a dead industry; there are open mine levels here that are dangerous to enter. This area is featured in Richard Adams' *The Plague Dogs*.

A path on the northern shore of the tarn leads to the reservoir access road and this is followed down, in scenes of increasing loveliness and thriving husbandry, to join the Walna Scar road before it meets the main valley road a pleasant half-mile north of Seathwaite. Dancing alongside in the final stages of the walk is Tarn Beck on its way to meet the River Duddon.

14 GRASSGUARDS, 1180'
Duddon Valley – Eskdale

FOR A WALK of sustained delight, the crossing of the broad ridge dividing the Duddon Valley and Eskdale must rank high in the itinerary of visitors enjoying a stay in the southern part of Lakeland. The start and finish are amid scenery of idyllic loveliness, sadly marred by recent extensive conifer plantations on the Duddon flank of Harter Fell but the forest so created is skirted rather than entered and does not detract from the pleasures of a summer walk.

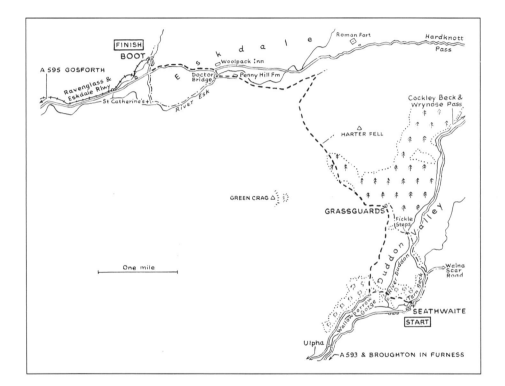

THE ISOLATED BUILDINGS of Grassguards may be reached by either of two routes from the Duddon Valley. From Seathwaite church a path leads through woodlands, crossing Tarn Beck, to a bridge that has replaced stepping stones on the River Duddon in a setting joyful to behold: here the river is seen issuing from the steep confining slopes of Wallowbarrow Gorge, a ravine bedecked with heather and trees, and always a place of bewitching beauty. Over the bridge, the path turns west to join a cart-track used by the scattered farms hereabouts and this climbs steadily to open countryside and Grassguards.

The alternative route leaves the road a mile north of Seathwaite and crosses a pasture to reach the river, where the huge stepping stones of Fickle Steps admit to the wooded slope on the far bank. This too is a charming spot although the crossing may cause some apprehension. Safely accomplished, a path rises through native trees to emerge at Grassguards.

Opposite *From the bridge in Wallowbarrow Gorge*

Upper Eskdale from Harter Fell; Hardknott Fort is visible in the centre

---

From Grassguards, the path heads north-west, with open undulating country on the left and, when the trees are left behind, the beckoning pyramid of Harter Fell rising in colourful slopes. An insignificant watershed is crossed, marked by a broken wall, and Eskdale starts to take shape ahead. When a track branches off, obviously bound for the summit of Harter Fell, the ascent of this fine mountain should be considered: the climb, amongst heather, is rewarded with fine views of Eskdale, the summit is exciting, the highest inches reached only by simple scrambling up naked rock. The northern panorama of the head of Eskdale, backed by the Scafells and Bowfell, with a nearer aerial view of Hardknott Roman Fort, is truly magnificent. If two parties have arranged to do the walk from opposite directions, it needs to be discussed beforehand whether Harter Fell is to be included; if so, the summit makes a grand meeting place.

Resuming the main path and with Eskdale gloriously displaying its lovely plumage in front, descend into the valley. It is well to keep strictly to the path and not attempt short cuts on the lower slopes, since the bracken of Eskdale is the highest in the district and impenetrably dense. At the foot of the descent, a lane is joined and followed down-river, to pass Penny Hill Farm – a place of happy memories where I was first introduced to the life of a Lakeland farmer – and arriving at Doctor Bridge over the River Esk. The lane joins the valley road near the Woolpack Inn, and the village of Boot is a short mile to the left.

But to enjoy some delectable river scenery, an enchanting path leaves Doctor Bridge and follows the Esk down-river as it rounds a wooded hill and leads to St Catherine's church, the parish church of Eskdale, a plain structure built in the seventeenth century and more remarkable for the contents of the graveyard than for those of the interior. Here is Tommy Dobson's grave, marked by a headstone inscribed with his own likeness, a fox, a hound and horn: a masterpiece in granite. Tommy's name has not lived on as has John Peel's, yet his local reputation as a Master of Foxhounds was even greater. Foxhunting was his whole life and his memorial reflects this passion.

A lane from the church leads to journey's end in the friendly village of Boot.

Tommy Dobson's grave
Below left and right *Penny Hill Farm*

Above *Far Easedale*

Below *Greenup Gill*

15 GREENUP EDGE, 1995'
Grasmere – Borrowdale

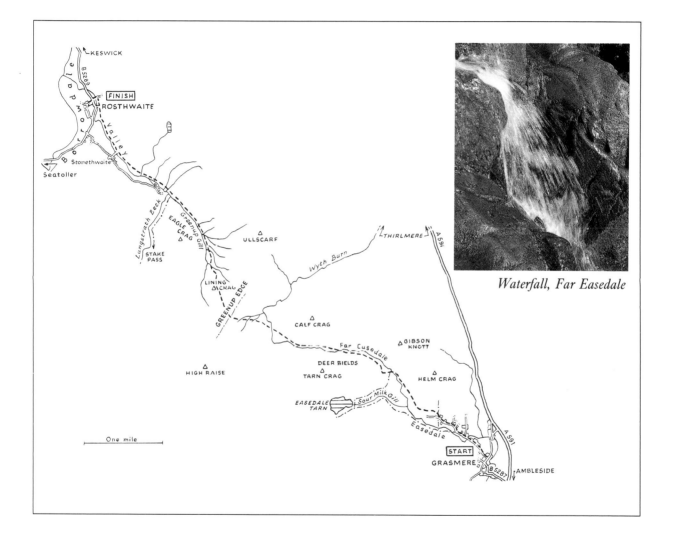

Waterfall, Far Easedale

TRAVELLERS ON FOOT between Grasmere and Borrowdale have little choice of route if they seek the shortest and most direct way. The central mass of fells must be crossed at a high level and the key to the easiest passage is Greenup Edge, a gap on the ridge joining High Raise and Ullscarf but, unfortunately for many walkers who have gone astray, not an obvious one when approached from Grasmere. The Edge is wild and lonely and provides a sharp contrast with the initial and final stages of the walk which are verdant and beautiful. Greenup Edge links two of the most popular parts of Lakeland and is in daily use.

LEAVE GRASMERE by the road to Easedale, from which a very popular path turns off to cross Easedale Beck and climb by the side of Sour Milk Gill, a delightful cataract, to Easedale Tarn. This is a prime objective of most sojourners at Grasmere – even in Victorian times when refreshments could be obtained at a stone hut near the outflow, but this has gone and today's visitors must take their own picnic lunches.

The route to Borrowdale, however, still with a tarmac surface, follows the main valley into Far Easedale, passing some desirable residences, and from it another well-trodden path leads upwards to another much visited objective, Helm Crag. This is better known as the Lion and the Lamb, to which the summit rocks bear a fancied resemblance.

These off-route attractions have no place in the itinerary of walkers bound for Borrowdale. The road is continued to its extremity where it becomes a rough lane alongside Far Easedale Beck which, when the last walls are passed, is crossed at Stythwaite Steps to a path heading upstream in open country. The path is unmistakable and cannot be lost even in mist, the sound of rushing water giving direction. Up on the left is the formidable Deer Bields Buttress, jutting from the lofty ridge that divides the two Easedales; on the right are the colourful slopes of Gibson Knott, continuing the skyline from Helm Crag. In places, the path crosses marshy ground where bog asphodel is rampant and then, after a rocky scramble, reaches the watershed marking the head of the valley of Far Easedale.

Looking towards Grasmere from the Easedale Tarn path

Easedale Tarn

Below *Summit of Greenup Edge*

The head of Far Easedale was formerly crossed by a wire fence of which a forlorn iron stepstile is the sole remaining relic. Beyond, the ground declines to a valley draining to the right, and walkers under the mistaken belief that the watershed is Greenup Edge may descend in that direction thinking it will lead down to Borrowdale. It won't: this is the valley of Wythburn going down to the head of Thirlmere, nowhere near Borrowdale, and containing extensive tracts of marshy ground indicated on Ordnance maps as The Bog. Greenup Edge is still half a mile distant and at a higher level; it can be discerned in front, slightly to the left of the ridge declining from the facing fell of Ullscarf. The path to it declines gently at first and then rises steadily, crossing several streams draining into Wythburn.

The path over Greenup Edge is a simple promenade on easy ground between the rough declivities of High Raise on the left and the smoother slopes of Ullscarf on the right, and either of these summits may be climbed from this point by walkers with energy to spare. But most will go forward for the distant glimpse of the Borrowdale heights and a bird's-eye view of the valley of Greenup Gill curving steeply down on the next stage of the journey.

With the flat top of the Edge left behind, the path starts the long descent, soon bypassing the rocky upthrust of Lining Crag and coming alongside Greenup Gill and fording the many tributaries joining in from Ullscarf. The descent continues below the cliffs of Eagle Crag (the best known of a dozen Eagle Crags in Lakeland, all named when golden eagles were resident in the district in past centuries) and out of its shadow reaches valley level at a lovely watersmeet where Langstrath Beck joins Greenup Gill from a wide opening on the left. Great slabs of rock are a feature of the confluence and they are a much favoured halting place. A drowning tragedy here is commemorated by a memorial bridge.

Right *Lining Crag*
Greenup Gill meets Langstrath Beck

Eagle Crag from Stonethwaite Beck

The finish of the walk is along the Stonethwaite Valley directly ahead, a mile of exquisite beauty where the distinctive charm of Victorian Lakeland is still preserved. Out of sight and sound of the Borrowdale traffic, the Stonethwaite Valley is an Arcadia of delight, its huddle of cottages and farm buildings an architectural gem, and living a life unchanged for centuries. The environs of wooded fellsides, sparkling streams and emerald pastures make Stonethwaite, in my opinion, the most charming of Lakeland's side valleys. Nothing is orderly as modern planners would have it; a carefree untidiness pervades the scene and hits exactly the right key in bewitching enchantment. The whole is an epitome of rural peace and serenity in a landscape of romance. Here is a surviving example of Lakeland's unique charm that has to such a large extent been destroyed by the very same people who come in search of it.

The path ends in the busy main street of Rosthwaite, a metropolis after Stonethwaite. Here, back in civilisation, advantage can be taken of the Borrowdale bus to go to Keswick for a connection to Grasmere if it is desired to return to the starting point of the walk. It must be grudgingly conceded that despite the damage done to the twentieth-century Lakeland scene by the internal combustion engine, buses can sometimes be a blessing.

16 GRISEDALE HAUSE, 1929'
Grasmere – Patterdale

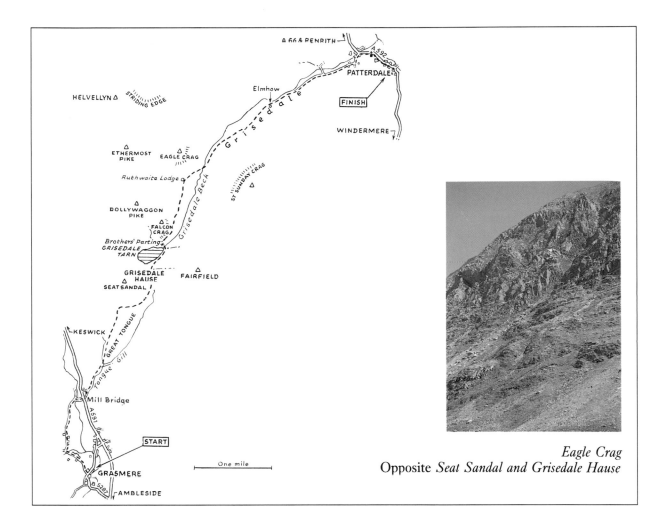

Eagle Crag
Opposite *Seat Sandal and Grisedale Hause*

THE ROYAL ROAD for walkers journeying between Grasmere and Patterdale lies over Grisedale Hause, and indeed there is no other direct way that does not call for serious climbing. It is a route used for centuries by the dalesmen and later adopted in part for the ascent of Helvellyn when the fashionable method of reaching the summit was on the backs of ponies.

It is a splendid walk through the mountains in contrasting scenery, beautiful at the extremities and grimly austere in its higher sections, and is much used as a springboard for the ascent of the many popular heights that flank the route.

With the possible exceptions of the Sty Head and Rossett passes, Grisedale Hause may well be the most trodden of the high crossings amongst the fells that are and will always remain the exclusive preserve of travellers on foot.

Above *Grisedale Tarn*

Below *The Vale of Grasmere from Grisedale Hause*

A SIGNPOST on the A591 at Mill Bridge, just above the Travellers' Rest, points the way along a pleasant lane with Tongue Gill in close company. This ends when confronted by a steep conical slope that seems to bar further progress. This is Great Tongue, Tongue being a name common in Lakeland where a sharp upthrust of land divides a valley into two parallel descending sections. But here, as in most such cases, paths go round the obstacle on both sides. The left fork is usually taken, this being the way the ponies went, and the breast of Seat Sandal is ascended on a grass path before contouring to the stony rise below the hause. The right fork is easier initially but terminates in a steep rough scramble alongside waterfalls to join the other. The final rise to the hause is short but arduous on loose stones. At the crest, crossed by a sturdy wall, fine views fore and aft reward earlier effort.

The outlet of Grisedale Tarn

Ahead, Grisedale Tarn comes suddenly into view, backed by the featureless slopes of Dollywaggon Pike, up which winds a well-worn and dusty track; this was the former pony route to Helvellyn but nowadays is usually littered by countless humans, some struggling upwards, many fallen by the wayside. On the right beyond the tarn rise the even steeper slopes of St Sunday Crag, and between the two heights is the V-shaped gap that contains the valley of Grisedale. It is a barren landscape that greets the walker at Grisedale Hause, but look back to see, in total contrast, the verdant Vale of Keswick, Coniston Water and the undulating lesser fells of southern Lakeland.

From the hause, tracks go off to Seat Sandal, left, and Fairfield, right, but the main route goes forward, descending slightly to the outlet of the tarn, this being easily forded; here the path to Helvellyn turns left and the pass route to Patterdale follows the direction of the issuing stream, Grisedale Beck.

A short distance below the outlet, on a slope littered by fallen boulders is one of special significance; this is an inscribed boulder known as the Brothers' Parting, marking the spot where William Wordsworth said a last farewell to his brother John in 1805. They never met again, John being drowned in the ship he commanded shortly afterwards.

The path goes forward into Grisedale, descending slightly at first and revealing the shadowed cliffs of Falcon Crag high on the left before reaching a solitary stone hut, Ruthwaite Lodge, built originally as a shooting lodge but taken over by a mountaineering club. The stream cascading down the fellside nearby deserves a second glance: note the old mine level at the side.

From Ruthwaite Lodge the path descends more steeply to the floor of the valley, again crossing Grisedale Beck. Up on the left is the near-vertical precipice of Eagle Crag, a haunt not of eagles but of rockclimbers. Towering on the right are the un-remitting slopes of St Sunday Crag, nearly 2000 feet above and topped by a fringe of cliffs down which a woman fell to her death recently after going astray on the summit of the mountain.

From here on the walking is easy, the path becoming a cart-track and affording impressive retrospects of Dollywaggon Pike which now assumes the form of a slender pyramid, and neighbouring Nethermost Pike, starkly etched against the sky above a line of crags.

Above *Ruthwaite Lodge*

Below left *Eagle Crag*   and right *Nethermostcove Beck*

Grisedale

Below *Patterdale church*

In scenery of increasing loveliness, the first buildings are reached at the farm of Elmhow. I once spent a night in a barn here without permission. The occasion was Coronation Day 1953, a public holiday, and I arrived at dusk after walking over the tops from Ambleside. I found a comfortable bed of straw but, being apprehensive of discovery, was unable to sleep and chain-smoked through the hours of darkness (I was on cigarettes in those days) without setting the barn on fire. I was off at dawn before the farmer started his morning rounds. I had to be in Kendal at nine o'clock to open the office, and walked over to Grasmere to catch the first morning bus. The day was memorable because it brought the news that Hillary and Tensing had reached the summit of Everest, an event that interested me more than the Coronation, for I had long cherished an impossible ambition to be the first man to reach the top of the highest mountain in the world. The news effectively burst a silly bubble.

Further down the valley, the cart-track becomes a tarmac road used as an unofficial parking place for the cars of motorists who take to their legs for the ascent of Helvellyn by way of Striding Edge. The road leads down through an avenue of trees to join the A592 near Patterdale church, the village and refreshments for which the body has been clamouring being around the corner to the right.

The A592 has infrequent bus services and wise people wishing to avail themselves of these facilities will have studied the timetables in advance and kept an eye on their watches.

17 HARDKNOTT PASS, 1290'
Duddon Valley – Eskdale

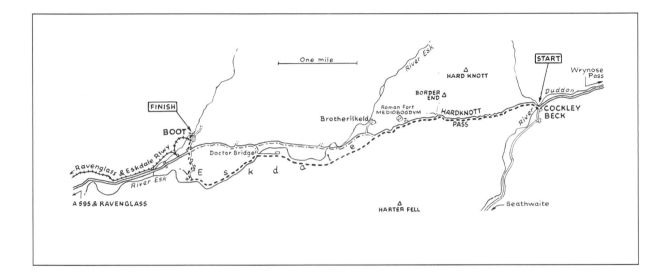

SEVEN OF THE mountain passes in Lakeland are crossed by motor roads, all of them having steep gradients on both sides, but quite the most notorious, challenging the skill and nerve of car drivers, is Hardknott Pass between the Duddon Valley and Eskdale.

Hardknott is almost a twin to Wrynose and usually both passes are crossed on the same journey, but motorists who have come over Wrynose from the east must expect a much stiffer climb over Hardknott and should approach it with the utmost concentration. It is no place for learner drivers. Height is not the problem, the altitude at the top being modest and lower than most of the others: it is the steepness of certain sections. Even the Romans baulked at the steepest part and sacrificed pride and principles by adopting a detour to circumvent the difficulties.

Opposite *The top of Hardknott Pass*
Right *The Scafell range from Border End*

THE ROAD STARTS to climb innocuously from the River Duddon at Cockley Beck Bridge but soon springs to life in a heart-stopping series of sharp and narrow hairpin bends with a gradient of 1 in 3, without respite until an easier incline to the top of the pass is reached. It is not unusual to find cars and their owners stranded on the unenclosed verges, or halted for breath on the more accommodating summit. Over the pass, with a glorious view of Eskdale ahead, there is a steep and awkward corner to negotiate before the road settles down in a long decline to the valley.

Towards the end of this descent, on an elevation to the right of the road, is the best preserved of the Roman forts in Lakeland: this is Mediobognvm, commonly referred to as Hardknott Castle, and should certainly be visited. Dating from the second century and identified beyond doubt by inscribed stones and

discoveries on the site, the fort is a pattern of drystone walls, some partly restored, with four gateways, the complex comprising the commandant's house, the barracks of the garrison, a granary and bath houses, while on the fellside above was a parade ground. Imagination is needed to comprehend the scale of the encampment and to appreciate the lonely life of the soldiers exiled here, far from home. Mediobognvm was of strategic importance to the Romans, defending the approach from the coast at a point of great vantage. It is in the care of English Heritage.

Above *Cockley Beck Bridge*

Hardknott Fort

Returning to the road, the descent continues to the floor of the valley, occupied by the River Esk and generously endowed with lush fields and lovely trees, and goes on to the village of Boot amidst scenery of unspoilt charm. At Boot, a miniature railway makes a delightful seven-mile journey to connect with the main line at Ravenglass.

Walkers over Hardknott Pass have little chance of escaping from the traffic on the Duddon side, the verges being too rough and boggy for easy progress, but upon reaching the top they should leave the road and scramble higher to the crest of Border End for a magnificent prospect of the Scafells and Bowfell and the other wild mountains circling upper Eskdale. After visiting the Roman fort, they should proceed down the valley by footpath from the bottom of the hill, enjoying the idyllic surroundings of the River Esk flowing nearby. At Doctor Bridge, the road may be joined for the last mile to Boot or, pleasanter, the river may be followed around a wooded hill on an enchanting path to the humble parish church of Eskdale, where the remarkable memorial to Tommy Dobson in the graveyard should be inspected (*see* page 73). A short lane then leads to the village.

Above *Remains of Hardknott Fort*

Eskdale

18 HART CRAG COL, 2520′
Rydal – Deepdale

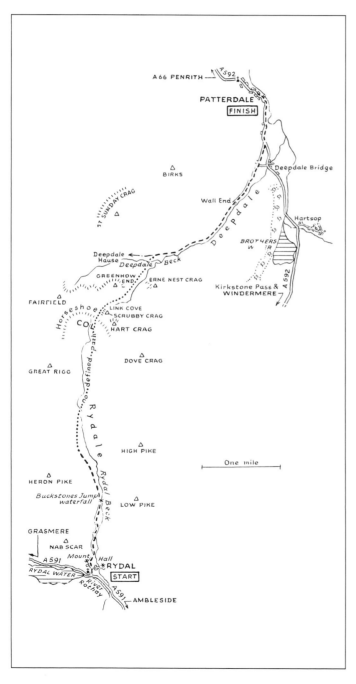

A66 PENRITH → ·A592·
PATTERDALE
FINISH
BIRKS △
Deepdale Bridge
St SUNDAY CRAG
Wall End
Deepdale
Hartsop
BROTHERS WR
Deepdale Hause
Deepdale Beck
GREENHOW END
ERNE NEST CRAG △
FAIRFIELD △
Horseshoe
COL
LINK COVE
SCRUBBY CRAG
HART CRAG △
Kirkstone Pass & WINDERMERE
A592
DOVE CRAG △
GREAT RIGG △
Rydale
undefined path
HIGH PIKE △
Rydal Beck
One mile
HERON PIKE △
Buckstones Jump waterfall
LOW PIKE △
GRASMERE
NAB SCAR △
Mount Hall
A591
RYDAL
START
RYDAL WATER
River Rothay
A591
→ AMBLESIDE

A N EXCEPTION to the general rule that the passes offer simple walking is provided by the abrupt gap, formerly known as The Step, on the ridge linking Hart Crag and Fairfield. It is not the actual crossing of the gap that is arduous, but the approaches to it, especially on the Rydale side, and walkers who like to preserve a dignified bearing will not enjoy the steep and stony scramble to reach the crest. It is, however, the most direct way across the high range dividing the Rothay valley at Rydal from Deepdale and Patterdale; it is the shortest in distance but not in time. The route has other merits, too, being unfrequented, remote from traffic, and pleasantly approached from either side on easy paths, only the middle mile calling for strenuous effort.

Opposite *Fairfield*
Below *Head of Rydale*

RYDAL IS LEFT by a side road from the A591, passing between the church and Rydal Mount on the left and Rydal Hall on the right, initially negotiable by cars. This soon degenerates into a rough lane and then a path; when clear of trees, there is a comprehensive view of the Fairfield Horseshoe ahead. The long valley opening in front is conveniently but unofficially known as Rydale. The surroundings are impressive and become more so as the walk proceeds up the valley alongside a wall, with Rydal Beck flowing nearby; there is a minor interruption at the small waterfall of Buckstones Jump. The dominant height in a lofty skyline is Great Rigg, falling in a rough declivity, and beyond this the valley is terminated by the high barrier of Fairfield and Hart Crag, the gap between them being the next objective. The hard work starts when the wall turns away and the path fades to nothing. The ground rises ahead and soon becomes unremittingly steep, upward progress not being helped by the absence of a path. The only guidance is given by the infant Rydal Beck which should be crossed and kept on the left during the final ascent. After a long and arduous struggle against gravity, the col is gained suddenly and with profound relief.

Rydale

Deepdale from the col

Although both sides of Hart Crag Col are virgin, untrodden and silent, the narrow crest has been blazed white by thousands of boots each year engaged on the very popular Fairfield Horseshoe walk, this spot being the only place where deviations are ruled out by the ruggedness of the terrain. It is also the most spectacular. The Rydal side has no terrors other than steepness and indeed has a tranquil view, but the Deepdale side has a fearsome aspect of wild country flanked by crags.

This is a true col, a narrow causeway poised above steep and inhospitable acclivities. The walk continues down a bouldery slope without the help of a foot-track, but the gradient eases as a way is made below the impending cliffs of Scrubby Crag. A stream joins the route of descent as it issues from the hanging valley of Link Cove, and takes over as guide on the next part of the walk.

Again the ground steepens as the stream plunges in cascades to the floor of the valley, passing below the tremendous buttress of Greenhow End in the shadow of Erne Nest Crag to join Deepdale Beck as it emerges from the wild recesses of Fairfield. This is a lonely place indeed: a silent sanctuary almost encircled by steep fellsides and dark crags with only the stream to point a way of escape. The vast sprawling slopes of St Sunday Crag fill the background as the waters of the beck are forded to gain the comfort of a path running above the far bank. Looking back from this point, the great tower of Greenhow End is seen as the impressive termination of the northern precipices of Fairfield.

Greenhow End

The rest is easy. The path curves around the base of St Sunday Crag and gradually the scene becomes less confined as trees, walls and cultivated fields mark the final stages of Deepdale. Across the beck flowing alongside rises the high but declining ridge of Hartsop above How, ending in woodlands above Brothers Water; on the left the steep and craggy slopes of St Sunday Crag and Birks rise to heaven. At the first farm of Wall End, the path merges into a lane with a few scattered houses, reaching the A592 near Deepdale Bridge. Patterdale village is a mile along the road to the left; a beautiful finish.

Above *View down Deepdale to Bridge End*

Deepdale Bridge

19 HAUSE GATE, 1150′
Newlands – Manesty

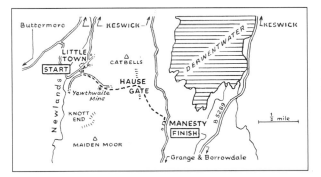

HAUSE GATE is a favourite objective although not well known by name. It is easily reached on a summer evening's stroll, rewarding the small effort with views of surpassing beauty. Everybody knows Catbells. The Hause (there is no gate, the word here meaning an open passage) is the grassy saddle on the ridge south of this popular summit, and is a place to halt awhile and try to memorise a scene to relive during moments of urban depression.

NEWLANDS IS LEFT at the hamlet of Little Town where an old mine road branches left and rises below the cliffs of Knott End to an area despoiled by the disused Yewthwaite Mine where there are still dangerous shafts and levels that call for caution if being explored, having already accounted for a fatal casualty. Beyond, the path rises in bracken to the top of the ridge at Hawes Gate, revealing a ravishing view of Derwentwater and its environs: a picture to bring tears of joy. A delectable grass path descends the fellside, every step a pleasure to tread, but there is such an eye-catching view ahead that it is advisable to halt on the uneven path when surveying the glorious scene.

At Manesty, the west Derwentwater road is joined and can be followed on to Grange in Borrowdale and its bus service.

Opposite *Derwentwater from Hause Gate*　　　　Below *Borrowdale from Hause Gate*

20 HIGH TOVE, 1665'
Thirlmere – Borrowdale

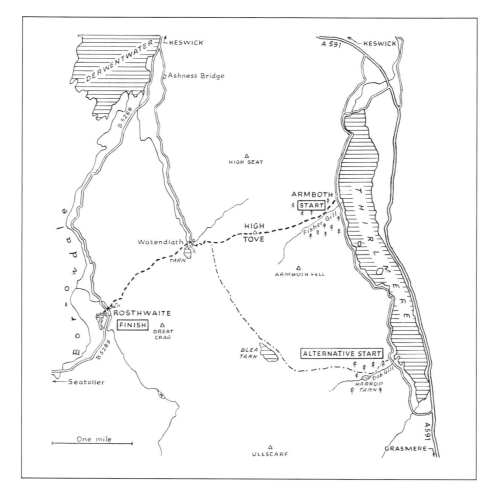

THERE ARE TWO paths along which walkers may cross the long central ridge that divides the Thirlmere valley and Borrowdale. One, giving a fine walk, leaves the west side of Thirlmere at Dob Gill near the south end of the reservoir, passes through the plantations around Harrop Tarn and crosses the indefinite ridge to descend to Watendlath by way of Blea Tarn. But this route is more in the nature of a cross-country walk than a pass.

The other path leaves the west side of Thirlmere near the north end of the reservoir and makes a beeline across the moorland of High Tove, actually visiting the summit, before descending to Watendlath. This route also hardly qualifies as a pass, traversing a low summit and not a depression, but passes over a watershed, being the most direct way, and has long been in use.

Opposite *Watendlath*

BEFORE MANCHESTER CORPORATION acquired rights to convert the natural lake of Thirlmere into a reservoir, Armboth House was the principal residence on the west shore, the centre of a small community connected to the east side by a picturesque wooden footbridge across the narrowest part of the lake. The house, other buildings and footbridge were all casualties of the reservoir and nothing was left of Armboth except its name, which curiously has survived on signposts. The slopes falling from the ridge have since been tightly afforested but directly above the site at Armboth a wide breach in the trees has been left unplanted to accommodate the old path over to Borrowdale. This climbs a bouldery slope alongside the plantation with outcropping rocks nearby and Fisher Gill in close attendance, and reaches a wall marking the upper limit of the plantations. The path passes through a gate and emerges on a wide moorland of heather and marsh, where it ascends more gradually to the cairned summit of High Tove, a place with no pretensions to interest or beauty, its one redeeming feature being as a viewpoint.

High Tove is a minor undulation on the long ridge forming the spine of central Lakeland. To the north, after a slight descent, the ground rises to High Seat; southwards, the nearest neighbour of note is Ullscarf, seen in the distance over the soggy morass of Armboth Fell. Over the watershed, the path descends gradually at first, and then, when Watendlath comes into sight ahead, much more steeply between two ravines, the gradient being eased by zigzags.

Watendlath is delightful and its qualities unique. There is no other place like it. A tiny cluster of white cottages and stone barns set at odd angles without pattern, a tarn, a stream and a bridge, all deeply inurned amongst surrounding fells and hidden from outside gaze: here are all the attributes of a perfect picture, a scene to enrapture artists and photographers. Apart from the intrinsic joys of this little hamlet in a fold of the hills, there are literary associations to attract visitors since this was the home of Judith Paris in the Herries novels by Hugh Walpole. Watendlath's link with the world outside is a narrow ribbon of tarmac branching from the Borrowdale road above Ashness Bridge, a three-mile journey of enchantment which, unfortunately, has been discovered by the touring motorist who often causes severe congestion. Watendlath should always be approached on foot; noise is sacrilege here. This is hallowed ground.

Watendlath Bridge

Watendlath is always left with regret and many a lingering look back. Sparing a crumb for the ducks, the walk is continued on a path that gets no rest from boots, and steadily climbs to the ridge that still hides Borrowdale; there are superb retrospective views of the hamlet and tarn on the way. This, if a census were taken, would be proved to be one of the most populated footpaths in Lakeland and, after topping the low ridge and starting the descent into Borrowdale, the reason for its popularity is clear. The upper reaches of this most beautiful of valleys unfold in a lovely pageant of colour and charm, the green strath and shaggy fells making a perfect canvas. With dragging steps, Rosthwaite is entered and the magic dispelled by tourist traffic.

Borrowdale

Below View towards Grisedale Pike from High Tove

21 HONISTER PASS, 1190′
Borrowdale – Buttermere

UNTIL THE MID-NINETEENTH century, when the turnpikes were improved for stagecoach traffic, and the railways came to Windermere and Keswick, the Lake District was a world apart, rarely visited by people from outside the area but, as early adventurers and the Lake Poets extolled its unique beauties, more were attracted to see for themselves. These were mainly professional gentlemen and their ladies.

In Victorian times, these visitors were conveyed in horse-drawn wagonettes on sightseeing tours along the few dusty and roughly metalled roads negotiable by wheeled vehicles, a romantic form of travel that vanished with the coming of tarmacadam and motor cars and omnibuses. Of these early tours, the great adventure, enjoyed on payment of a toll, was provided by the crossing of Honister Pass, a fearsome and exciting journey. Today the romance has been savaged out of existence by the procession of cars using this popular route linking Borrowdale and Buttermere, but the scenic grandeur of the past remains.

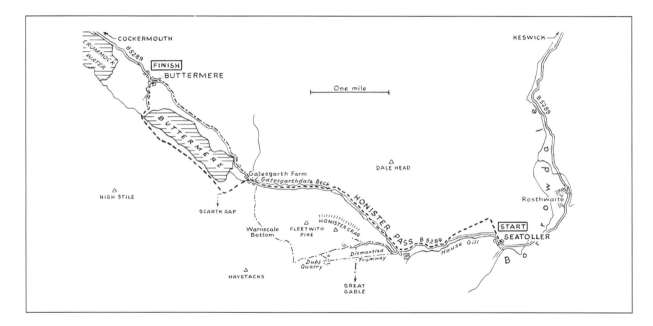

SEATOLLER IS THE bus terminus at the head of Borrowdale and from this attractive group of buildings the ascent to the pass starts at once and in earnest, the initial steepness being relieved by the sparkling cascades of Hause Gill alongside in a bower of trees, after which a bare landscape is entered as the unenclosed road rises more gently to the summit. Walkers can avoid most of the hard road to the top and the hazard of speeding cars by preferring the old toll road which is grassy, abandoned and much kinder to the feet: this branches off the road on the right after leaving Seatoller, and after a sharp turn heads directly for the pass at a higher level, joining the motor road below the top.

Opposite *Honister Pass*

Seatoller

Below *The cutting sheds, Honister Quarry*

Honister Pass is extremely impressive. The great feature is Honister Crag, a towering cliff honeycombed with quarries and a network of steep tracks used for bringing down the handsome slate that for colour, texture and durability has earned international renown. In the formative years of the industry, horse-drawn sleds were used to convey the blocks of slate to the cutting sheds; later a tramway served this purpose; this in turn was superseded by lorries making the perilous descent. Now all is silent: the centuries-old workings were closed recently and activity has come to an end. Honister Crag has had the heart torn out of it but has not been tamed.

There is a Youth Hostel on the top of the pass in addition to the quarry buildings, and limited space for the parking of cars; there is always activity here. It is a starting point for the ascent of Great Gable, using the old tramway, and on the north side an easy ridge can be climbed to the summit of Dale Head, where there is a classic view of Newlands and the Vale of Keswick backed by Skiddaw.

The High Stile range from Gatesgarth

Over the pass, the road descends steeply under a bridge built to carry a private cart-track from quarries on the side of Dale Head, and then winds down into a boulder-strewn defile. The gradient eases as Gatesgarthdale Beck comes alongside and a splendid view of the High Stile range unfolds ahead. The soaring slopes on the left gradually decline to valley level; a white cross on the lower rocks is a memorial to a girl accidentally killed here in 1887. The rugged crest of Haystacks appears in a wider landscape, and trees, welcome after the sterile crossing, enhance the majestic scene as the first habitation of Gatesgarth Farm is reached.

From Gatesgarth, the road continues for two lovely miles to Buttermere village with glimpses of the lake seen below. Walkers have a charming alternative on this final stage by following a lakeside path on the north-east side.

Fellwalkers who have a rooted objection to travelling along hard roads may follow a parallel course from the top of the pass by climbing up the old tramway on the left side and continuing on a good path skirting Dubs Quarry and descending to Gatesgarth along an old quarry road through Warnscale Bottom. This route is more arduous but in the matter of views better by far.

Kirkstone Pass looking north and (below) *south*

22 KIRKSTONE PASS, 1489'
Ambleside – Patterdale

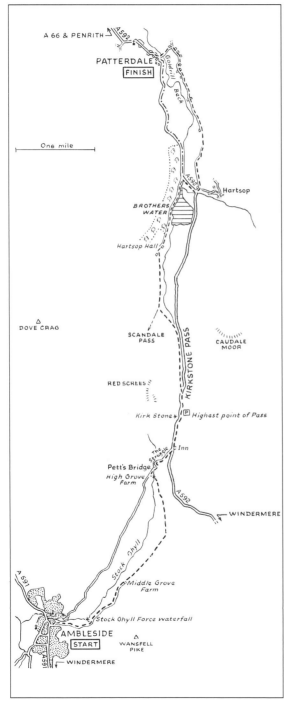

KIRKSTONE PASS is the high crossing that most excites the tourists who inspect the Lake District from the comfort of a car or coach. The environs of the pass are spectacular, a narrow road winding through a gap between the rugged downfall of Red Screes and the scree slopes of Caudale Moor. It is a wild defile of tumbled rocks and mountain debris, but the loneliness that characterised it a century ago, when horse-drawn carriages braved the rigours of the journey carrying parties of awestruck Victorians, has been dispelled by the procession of motorists who today throng the limited confines of the road. The atmosphere of frightening solitude has been lost and is fleetingly regained only when winter snowfalls block the pass.

A road climbs steeply to the summit from Ambleside, there joining the busy A592 from Windermere for the long descent to the Patterdale Valley. The weight of traffic on most days of the year makes this a route to be avoided by travellers on foot who would do well to favour instead the quiet and unfrequented track over Scandale Pass although this alternative bypasses Kirkstone's exciting scenery. However, the route described in this chapter enables walkers to make acquaintance with the pass on footpaths that avoid the motor road except for a long mile across the highest part. Even so, Kirkstone Pass is best appreciated when the summer visitors have departed.

LEAVE AMBLESIDE along the signposted road to Stock Ghyll Force, this delightful waterfall being seen by a walk through the woods alongside Stock Ghyll. In former days, an admission charge was made for the privilege of entry, but today access is free and a well-worn path leads up to the impressive plunge of the stream in a bower of foliage. It is a charming scene for Stock Ghyll Force is the most beautiful waterfall in the Lake District.

Near Middle Grove

The ruins near High Grove
Right *Red Screes*

A path above the fall leads back to the road which continues upstream to Middle Grove Farm along the lower flanks of Wansfell with Kirkstone Pass in sight ahead. Beyond the farm, a cart-track goes on to the ruins of High Grove Farm, from which a path crosses to join the motor road from Ambleside at Pett's Bridge. Originally the track went directly forward, climbing to join the A592. It is likely that this route by the Grove farms was the usual way to Kirkstone Pass before the road from Ambleside was constructed.

From Pett's Bridge, the motor road rises very steeply to the summit of the pass, this section being known as The Struggle for reasons that must have been very obvious when wheeled traffic was horse-drawn. At the top of this incline, the road meets the A592 at the Kirkstone Pass Inn, once known as the Travellers' Rest where there is an ample and well-patronised car park. This is a popular halt for refreshment or for gazing up at the formidable ramparts of Red Screes, up which there is a steep and arduous track from this point. The gentle slopes behind the inn provide simple ski runs when snow has been cleared from the road and cars can reach the inn. On a high shoulder of Caudale Moor overlooking the pass is a memorial cairn to Mark Atkinson, mine host at the inn for many years until his death in 1930.

The highest point of the pass is a short distance beyond the inn, and here a dramatic view forward is revealed, the long descent into Patterdale commences, the road being tightly enclosed between stone walls. A car park has been provided to discourage motorists from stopping on the edge of the road to admire the scene. Nearby is a massive fallen boulder, the Kirk Stone, from which the pass was named; its appearance on the skyline when approaching from the north resembles the steeple of a church tower. All around is chaotic convulsion of nature, a primeval desolation.

Opposite *The north side of Kirkstone Pass*   Above *Patterdale*

A signpost on the roadside lower down indicates a footpath along which pedestrians can escape from the hazards of speeding cars, this leading pleasantly down to valley level; there the path from Scandale Pass joins in. The walk proceeds, with views of Dove Crag, to Hartsop Hall, a farmhouse unusually distinguished by having a public right of way through the building as a result of the erection of an extension over a bridleway that formerly passed alongside.

A wooded lane continues the walk along the shore of Brothers Water, which was named Broad Water until two brothers lost their lives here by drowning on separate occasions early in the nineteenth century. The A592 is rejoined at the end of the lane and may be followed for two lovely miles to Patterdale village, but if traffic is heavy it is advisable to go back about 200 yards to the Hartsop junction, there taking a parallel and pleasant by-road where there is less danger of being annihilated by a car.

Thus ends an enjoyable ten-mile walk in contrasting surroundings, nature being displayed both in the raw and at its supreme best. For walkers already familiar with Kirkstone Pass, however, it is preferable to make the journey by way of Scandale Pass, which is innocent of wheels, rather shorter in distance, requires little more effort and is blessed with a profound solitude: *see* page 161.

23 THE LOFT BECK CROSSING, 1900′
Ennerdale – Borrowdale

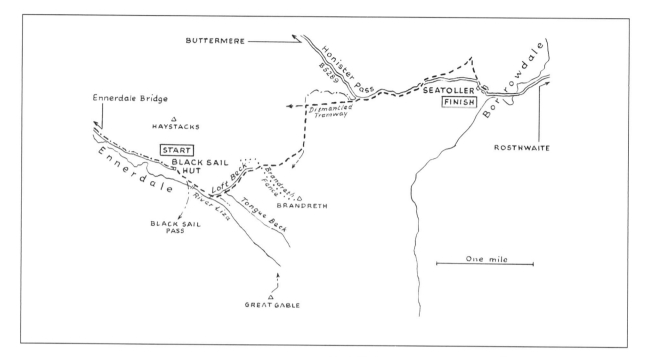

A USEFUL TIME-SAVING route between the Black Sail Hut in Ennerdale and Honister Pass is available by climbing up to the grassy plateau crossed by the Brandreth fence: this is a route not generally recognised as a pass but has the attributes if not the appearance of one. There is now a distinct track and this should be kept strictly underfoot in misty conditions, the highest part of the crossing being without landmarks. The track joins the broad path coming down from Great Gable for the descent to Honister Pass, from which the well-known delights of Borrowdale can be reached by an easy hour's march.

Left *Loft Beck*
Opposite *Great Gable from the River Liza*

A PATH FROM the Black Sail Hut goes up the valley of the River Liza towards Great Gable, ignoring the footbridge, to the point where the tributary of Loft Beck comes down steeply on the left. Loft Beck is the key to the route: it is followed up closely on a steep and rough track, passing a confluence of waters where Tongue Beck joins in, until the climbing ends on an extensive upland prairie. With Ennerdale now lost to sight behind, the path trends to the right across a grassy expanse with no distinctive features other than the old Brandreth fence, which is crossed to join the Great Gable path at a large cairn. Although the immediate environs are dreary and without interest, the views of the Buttermere fells and valley are of classical beauty.

Left *The Brandreth fence*
Below *The Buttermere fells*

Honister Pass

There are no problems of route finding when the Great Gable path is reached, this having been worn to the dimensions of a road, albeit a rough one, as the result of daily flagellation by countless boots. It goes easily down to the top of the old quarry tramway above Honister Pass and this is descended to the motor road on the summit of the pass.

Here, if continuing to Borrowdale, the road to the right leads down to Seatoller, and the bus terminus, but travellers on foot should, for the comfort of their feet, branch left along the old toll road, now no more than a grass cart-track, which reaches Seatoller much more pleasantly.

24 THE MARDALE CORPSE ROAD, 1670′
Mardale Head – Swindale

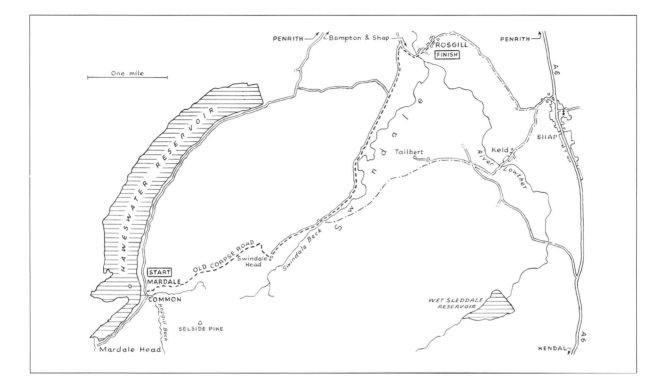

T HE EARLY SETTLERS in the Lake District, living in isolated communities amongst the fells, faced many problems, one of them being the disposal of their dead. Some had a church with burial rights nearby, but others had to devise routes across high country to the nearest consecrated ground. Such a community lived at Mardale Green, a lonely hamlet later to be drowned beneath Haweswater Reservoir in 1937. Before a church was built here in the seventeenth century, bodies were conveyed to Shap, eight miles distant, the coffins strapped to the backs of horses. The shortest way was due east, over Mardale Common, and is still known today as the Old Corpse Road.

Opposite *Mardale Head from the Old Corpse Road*
Right *The road around Haweswater Reservoir*

A STEEP PATH, rising in zigzags to ease the gradient, climbed directly from the little group of buildings at Mardale Green. It is probable that this path was engineered primarily as a sledgate for bringing peat down from Mardale Common, peat then being the main source of fuel, but it served the funeral corteges also and is best remembered for this purpose. The lower section of this path was engulfed and submerged by the reservoir, and a little higher is interrupted by the new road to Mardale Head which cuts across it, a signpost indicating the path's continuation up the fellside; this is the point at which modern walkers start the crossing to Swindale.

For several hundred feet the ascent is unremittingly steep, a series of delightful turns and twists, on a distinct path. Hopgill Beck nearby displays a long white ribbon of cascading waters: a pretty sight. Two roofless stone huts, built for the drying and storing of peat, are reached and then another.

The retrospective view of Mardale Head is superb, the encircling mountains appearing in fine array around the deep valley and presenting a scene that, in my opinion, is unrivalled in Lakeland. Above the huts, the steepness abates and the path continues as a narrow track across a wide grassy upland, reaching its highest point amidst undulating moors overtopped by Selside Pike. Then the path trends easily downhill into Swindale, reaching a road terminus at the farm buildings of Swindale Head.

Opposite *Swindale*
Below *Hopgill Beck*

This road goes down the valley, breasts a small hill where it is crossed by the Haweswater access road and descends to Rosgill, between Bampton and Shap. This is the end of the Mardale Head-Swindale pass but for the early mourners was only the first stage of their sad journey, Shap being still six miles distant, their route crossing Swindale and contouring around the facing fells to the last resting place at Shap.

It is interesting to note that when the church at Mardale Green was dismantled and demolished in 1936 as a casualty of the reservoir, the graves in the churchyard were exhumed and the coffins taken by an easier mode of transport to Shap for re-interment, thus reuniting the remains of the more recent dead with those of their ancestors who came the hard way along the Old Corpse Road.

This walk serves also as an introduction to Swindale, a quiet and lovely valley rarely visited by tourists and quite unspoilt. Swindale Beck did not escape the eyes of Manchester Corporation and its waters have been plundered, but thankfully unobtrusively and with little disturbance to the environment, being taken through a tunnel to augment Haweswater Reservoir.

25 MICKLEDORE, 2650'
Eskdale – Wasdale

MICKLEDORE IS the well-defined gap between Scafell and Scafell Pike crossed by a narrow ridge linking the two in a situation of awesome grandeur and amidst highly exciting rock scenery. I consider Mickledore to be the most impressive place in Lakeland: it compels attention to the exclusion of all else. Here is nature in the raw – savage, primeval, immense. In such surroundings man is a speck, insignificant and unimportant.

The ridge across the gap is short, the crest is narrow and the sides steep, and no deviations are possible from the blazed path along it. With towering crags at both ends, the gap is a natural pass yet the ridge is rarely used as such. The crossing from Eskdale to Wasdale Head is arduous. Why suffer all this effort when a simple walk by Burnmoor Tarn connects the two valleys? Almost invariably the Mickledore ridge is traversed by walkers passing between Scafell and Scafell Pike, this being the only feasible way from one to the other, and not as a pass between valleys, although in appearance it is the grandest pass of all.

Mickledore is high drama.

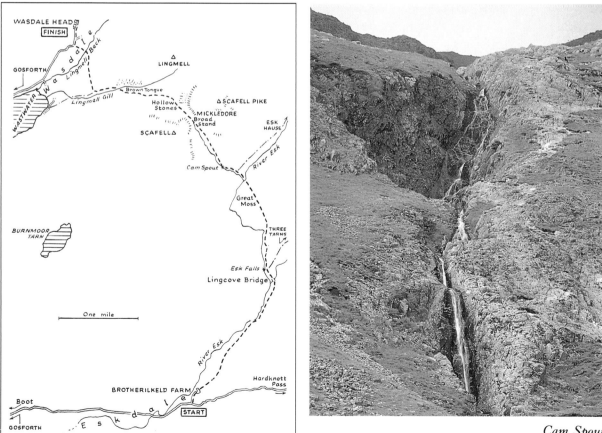

Cam Spout
Opposite *Mickledore*

WITH A FULL DAY ahead and emergency rations in the rucksack, the road along Eskdale is left near the foot of Hardknott Pass and the Esk followed upriver from Brotherilkeld Farm for two miles to Lingcove Bridge, spanning a tributary just above the confluence of waters. The main river here comes round a bend on the left, emerging from a deep gorge in which are the Esk Falls, a series of spectacular waterfalls and cataracts defying close access. The bridge is crossed to a path rising at a higher level in the same direction. The Scafells soon appear ahead, with Mickledore seen as a high gap on the skyline between the two giants in the range. The path continues easily to the foot of the tremendous mountain wall, crossing the flat and marshy expanse of Great Moss. The next objective is the slender waterfall of Cam Spout, this being reached after fording the Esk which is seen winding down from its headwaters below Esk Hause but is left behind at this point.

The ascent now starts in earnest up a steep path alongside Cam Spout. The stream pouring over the lip of the waterfall comes down from Mickledore and, ignoring tributaries joining from the left, gives direction to the remainder of the climb. Easier ground is reached above the waterfall, but the uphill trudge is relentless, flanked by the lower crags of Scafell and the stony slopes of Scafell Pike and in surroundings of extreme wildness and desolation. Timid pedestrians may well suffer apprehension as the track mounts higher towards even grimmer fastnesses ahead. An obvious gully opening on the left offers a scrambling route to the summit of Scafell by way of Foxes Tarn, but for Mickledore the route is directly ahead. It passes into the shadow of the vertical cliffs of Scafell's East Buttress and, beyond, the gaping mouth of Mickledore Chimney which, mercifully, does not have to be entered. Now on a treadmill of scree, with the gap of Mickledore close ahead, the final scramble is alongside a wall of crags split by two vertical cracks; the second, Fat Man's Agony, gives access to the notorious Broad Stand, a rockclimbers' short cut to Scafell but definitely not for lesser fry. After a few more slithering steps, the ridge is reached for a deserved halt.

I always find it difficult to tear myself away from Mickledore, always feel it a great privilege to be allowed admittance to such a wonderful place. Not because there is beauty here. The scene is brutal, uncompromising, yet fascinating and a little frightening. Massive towers of naked rock soar majestically into the sky on all sides. Here is nature's architecture, and it is overwhelming, reducing man to insignificance and a reverent humility. These vertical precipices are repelling: surely they could never be scaled? 'Nobbut a fleeing thing could get up theer,' said old Will Ritson a hundred years ago, yet since that time a network of climbing routes has been forged by expert pioneers on Scafell Crag and the neighbouring cliffs. Legs turn to jelly at the merest thought. Brave men, these, and I am not amongst them.

The Mickledore ridge is not razor-sharp nor a tightrope but is extremely narrow. Within two paces of reaching the crest, steps are immediately downhill on a funnel of scree, descending into a wild hollow below Scafell Crag, the most magnificent of Lakeland's cliffs, rising vertically on the left and far above. On the right, Pulpit Rock and Pikes Crag, outliers of Scafell Pike, enclose the amphitheatre effectively. There is grass here and many huge boulders, some of which offer crude shelter. This sanctuary is known as Hollow Stones.

Opposite *Scafell East Buttress from Mickledore*

Above *Hollow Stones*

Lingmell Beck and Wastwater

Wastwater

A night's bivouac in Hollow Stones is an experience long remembered. The hours of darkness are distinctly eerie, the impending crags around appearing as black silhouettes and the silence being that of the grave. Dawn brings a rich reward, the gloom gradually being dispell'd as the first rays of the sun touch the uppermost tips of Scafell Crag and then very slowly diffuse the whole rock face in a rosy pink glow.

But those who prefer a comfortable bed will continue easily down towards Wasdale, now in sight, passing the long fans of scree brought down from Scafell Pinnacle during a tremendous electric storm in 1958, overlaying earlier stonefalls. A path forms at the top of a long descending spur, Brown Tongue, this emerging from the claustrophobia of the crags and enjoying the wider landscape ahead.

At the foot of Brown Tongue, Lingmell Gill is forded, this also carrying the debris of a violent cloudburst, and the path rounds a corner to reveal splendid views of Wastwater and the patchwork fields of Wasdale Head backed by the Pillar range. With the latter prospect in view, the path descends to the valley, slanting down the breast of Lingmell End, a delightful finish to the day. Those who use Mickledore as a pass will never regret their choice over the soft option of Burnmoor. This has been a walk to remember and its memories will be evergreen.

26 MOOR DIVOCK, 1000'
Pooley Bridge – Helton

THE EASY CROSSING of Moor Divock would appeal not only to sedate walkers but also to those with archaeological and geological interests. The Moor is a wide grassy upland forming a broad saddle between Heughscar Hill where limestone is much in evidence, and the greater bulk of Loadpot Hill at the north end of the High Street range. At first sight, the moor seems to be a featureless expanse without landmarks, but appearances deceive. The bland surface of the ground abounds in surprises, but they are not obvious and need searching out. Moor Divock is in fact a rich field of exploration and discovery, a graveyard of relics of prehistoric occupation: stone circles, ancient cairns, burial mounds, settlements, standing stones and avenues. Here too is the famous Roman road, High Street, and even earlier than this is the wide path across the moor that probably originated in neolithic times. For the geologist, there are shakeholes and sinkholes galore, indicating a limestone bedrock, and for the simple walker a pleasant stroll amongst ghosts of the past. Moor Divock is history.

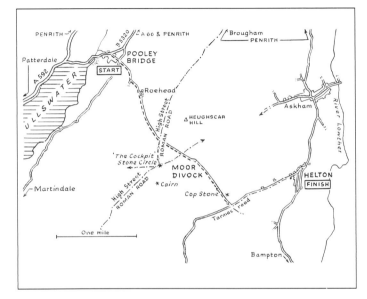

Opposite *Moor Divock*

The Roman Road

The stone circle

A LANE RISES south-east from Pooley Bridge, passing Roehead and reaching open country beyond, its continuation being a wide track, with branches to the left used by pony trekkers. The track ascends gently to a large cairn where it is crossed by the Roman road coming down from High Street on its way to Brougham. At this point, a recommended diversion follows the Roman road to the right, reaching a large stone circle alongside; about thirty yards in diameter and named on Ordnance maps as The Cockpit, it is worthy of leisurely inspection.

Returning to the main path, preferably by retracing steps to avoid the bogs met on short cuts, the walk is resumed, still ascending slightly and passing a line of shakeholes on the right. Near an old boundary stone, a path branches left for Askham. Ignoring this, the path goes on, in places as wide as a motor road. Across the moor on the right are the Pulpit Holes, a group of shakeholes which, on my first and only visit, were depositories for the carcasses and skeletons of sheep: this is not a diversion to be recommended! On the left side of the path reached by short detours is a series of small circles, cairns and burial mounds some of which have obviously been excavated or disturbed. These remains are not as complete as reported by nineteenth-century investigators, and it seems likely that some of the stones have been removed for use in the construction of shooting butts nearby: a double sacrilege.

Ahead on the skyline is a prominent upright boulder, the Cap Stone, thought to be a survivor of a former avenue of stones akin to the one at Shap and possibly a continuation of it. Just beyond, the path debouches on an unenclosed tarmac road, with wide verges often occupied by parked cars and this, followed to the left, leads down to the village of Helton, in the valley of the River Lowther.

This walk across Moor Divock, however, is so effortless and the path so pleasant that, on arrival at the tarmac, most walkers will simply turn round and return to Pooley Bridge the same way with the extra bonus of lovely views of Ullswater on the descent.

Above *A burial mound*

Above right *The Cap Stone* and below *Ullswater*

27 THE MOSEDALE WATERSHED, 1600'
Longsleddale – Swindale or Wet Sleddale

THERE ARE FIVE Mosedales in the Lake District, all of them justifying the interpretation of the name as 'Dreary Valley', and this one, the highest of them, is not merely dreary, but wild and lonely. It provides a crossing out of Longsleddale to Swindale or Wet Sleddale, passing between the high fells of Tarn Crag and Branstree, and was once in regular use but today is unfrequented and the path in parts has gone to seed.

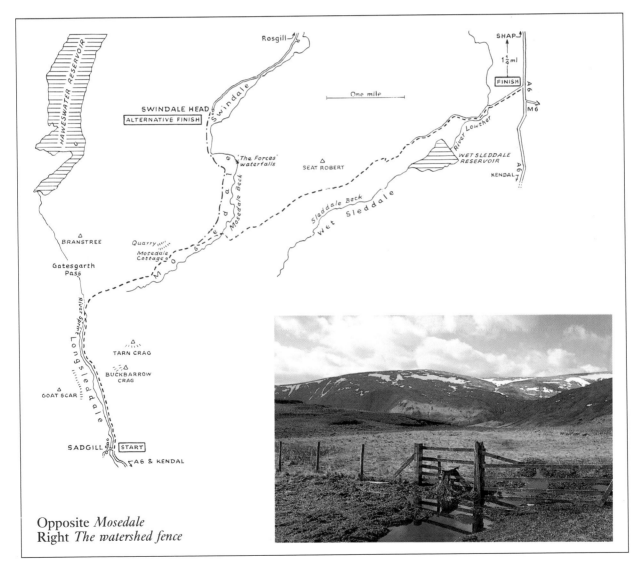

Opposite *Mosedale*
Right *The watershed fence*

FROM SADGILL BRIDGE in Longsleddale, where the motor road ends, a continuing cart-track goes forward into the head of the valley through a rocky portal formed by the cliffs of Goat Scar and Buckbarrow Crag. This section has many features of interest (described in the chapter on Gatescarth Pass, page 61). When the track escapes from its confining walls at a gate at the top of a steep rise, a path soon branches to the right from the Gatescarth route and aims for a wide depression in the skyline between the declining slopes of Tarn Crag and Branstree. The ascent to it is gentle; however, the original path, once of commercial use but now abandoned and taken over by nature, is obscure and interrupted by marshes as it rises to a gate in a wire fence crossing the depression. This is now seen to be a watershed as the ground beyond slowly declines and a new landscape appears ahead. The path goes on, indistinctly, across a vast grassy prairie for a further mile, maintaining a level contour. Mosedale Beck forms nearby, sluggishly confirming, against the visual evidence, that the watershed has indeed been crossed and the ground trending down. The path becomes clearer when a solitary building comes in sight: this is Mosedale Cottage, an overnight refuge for shepherds. On the fellside behind is the large disused Mosedale Quarry. These names confirm that we are now in Mosedale, although the bare and featureless terrain at such a high altitude bears little resemblance to a dale.

Mosedale Cottage and Quarry   *The Forces*

Wet Sleddale

Beyond the cottage, which is surely the loneliest in Lakeland, the path divides, the left branch contouring the slope and turning north with Mosedale Beck into Swindale. In the later stages of the descent, the beck provides a display of waterfalls known as The Forces before the road terminus is reached at the farm buildings of Swindale Head.

The main branch goes ahead to cross Mosedale Beck at a primitive bridge as its waters drain north into Swindale. The facing slope is rounded and then follows a long and gradual descent into Wet Sleddale on a distinct track, once a cart road but later reduced to the status of a bridleway. Wet Sleddale is a long deep valley flanked by lesser fells and its details are well seen from the track which maintains a high level above it. Down in the bottom of the valley may be discerned the stone walls, 12 feet high, of a medieval deer trap, unique in the district. Further on is the new Wet Sleddale Reservoir, Manchester's latest and hopefully last, with its attendant casualties of ruined buildings and broken walls.

The track slants down to valley level, becoming tarred to serve the remaining active farms; it passes a Victorian postbox set in a wall before crossing the River Lowther to join the A6 a mile south of Shap.

Nobody will rank the crossing of this Mosedale amongst the best of Lakeland passes, much of it being dull and unexciting, and Wet Sleddale has an atmosphere of forlorn sadness, but on a day of fine weather it provides a satisfactory nine-mile walk.

28 MOUSTHWAITE COMB, 1350'
Scales – Mungrisdale

A SHORT AND simple pass walk is available on the eastern fringe of the Northern Fells, crossing a low col to enter the little-known valley of the River Glenderamackin and passing below the long escarpment of Bannerdale Crags before reaching the village of Mungrisdale. It is a pleasant expedition in unfrequented terrain, requiring little effort and suitable for a short half-day after a morning's rain.

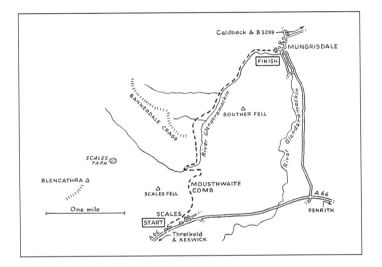

FROM THE HAMLET of Scales on the A66 east of Threlkeld starts a popular path over Scales Fell to Blencathra, skirting a hollow in the fells known as Mousthwaite Comb.

Crossing this hollow and ignoring the well-trodden path up Scales Fell and another branching left to Scales Tarn, the head of the hollow is reached at a col on the east side, whence a descending path slants down to a bridge over the River Glenderamackin and joins another path on the far bank.

The course of the Glenderamackin is interesting, suggesting an early problem in deciding the direction of flow. From its source, it heads south-east, turns east on finding its way barred by Mousthwaite Comb, is then turned north by Souther Fell and when the latter declines to valley level flows east through Mungrisdale and then due south and finally west to join the River Greta, almost completing a circuit of Souther Fell.

Across the river rises the long southern slope of Bannerdale Crags, and the path on the far bank contours round its base, following the river as it turns north and soon bringing into view the mile-long escarpment of Bannerdale Crags. These are palpably inaccessible except at one point where a steep ridge comes down to the valley, yet has ruins of old mines high amongst the cliffs. When the river turns east, a tributary beck is forded and an improving path, becoming a lane, leads into the attractive small village of Mungrisdale, two miles by road from the A66 and its bus service.

Opposite *Blencathra from Mousthwaite Comb*

29 NAN BIELD, 2100'
Kentmere – Mardale

OF ALL THE Lakeland passes, I rank
Nan Bield amongst the finest. It con-
forms most to my concept of a true mountain
pass or col, being delicately sculptured,
narrow at its crest and steeply descending on
both sides. It is poised high, a lonely gap
between lofty fells, and retains features from
long ago when it served as a trade route for
packhorses. Unmarred by wheeled traffic,
this is a way only for travellers on foot and
wearing stout boots.

Nan Bield provides a direct link between
the Kentmere valley and Mardale, and six
miles of rough and in places steep ground
separate their road termini. The road to
Kentmere leaves the A591 at Staveley,
midway between Kendal and Windermere:
the A591 is the usual approach to the Lake
District from the south and the turn to
Kentmere is often overlooked or, being a
dead end, ignored by motorists hurrying to
reach Windermere which, for many of them,
marks the start of Lakeland. The four miles
to the little community of Kentmere are
consequently relatively quiet and mainly
used by local traffic and the discerning few
who disagree that Lakeland starts at
Windermere. These four miles along a
winding valley are lovely, the River Kent
pursuing a rapid course through pleasant
pastures and woodlands where daffodils and
bluebells are a springtime delight. Of course
Lakeland doesn't start at Windermere; here
in the Kentmere valley, natural charm typical
of the district is all around and no less
enchanting. Here romance is allied to beauty.

Opposite *Nan Bield*

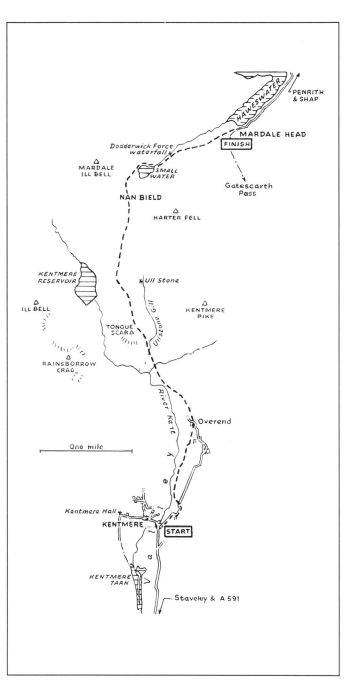

Unlike the neighbouring Longsleddale, the Kentmere valley curves, revealing a succession of fresh scenes and occasional sightings of the mountains ahead. After passing a former asbestos works, open ground is reached and there is a distant view of the church on a hill. Across fields is the new Kent Mere. On the flat strath south of the church was formerly a shallow lake, the Kent Mere that gave its name to the valley and village. This was drained in 1840 to provide more land for cultivation – a purpose not entirely achieved, much of the reclaimed ground remaining too marshy for the plough and for grazing. Analysis of the former bed of the lake in the present century disclosed the presence of rich deposits of diatomaceous earth which, when extracted and processed, proved a valuable insulation material and led to the establishment of a works on the site. During these operations, the remains of two primitive boats in the form of dugout canoes, believed to be of the Viking period, were discovered; the better of the two specimens is now at the National Maritime Museum. The draining of the lake in 1840 was probably a factor in the erratic flow of the river that led to the promotion of an Act of Parliament to create a reservoir in the upper reaches of the valley. Today, with supplies of diatomaceous earth exhausted and the industry closed, a new Kent Mere has come into being on the same site: a narrow sheet of water half a mile in length.

Nearby is the site of an ancient British village settlement and the valley has other evidences of prehistoric occupation. Not far from the church is Kentmere Hall, with a ruined fourteenth-century pele tower: this was the birthplace in 1517 of Bernard Gilpin, who had a distinguished career in the Church and became known as 'The Apostle of the North'.

Rainsborrow Crag

Ill Bell and Kentmere Reservoir   *Southern approach to Nan Bield*

THE ROADS in the village are narrow and unsuitable for the parking of cars: it is usual to take advantage of an open space alongside the church. The way to Nan Bield, now on foot, starts from the bridge where the Low Bridge Inn was formerly. Here turn up a side road heading north until a signpost (to Mardale) indicates a path with the River Kent nearby rushing through a tree-lined gorge in a series of cataracts and waterfalls. The footpath leads to the farm buildings of Overend, the last outpost of civilisation, and continues beyond, passing a quaint bridge used for access to fields across the river. The scenery now is very impressive, the dominant feature being Rainsborrow Crag on the other side of the valley, backed by Ill Bell and its satellites. On the right, colourful slopes rise to Kentmere Pike, 1600 feet above. Ahead, blocking the valley, is Tongue Scar, a craggy upthrust at the foot of which are long-established badger setts. The river curves to the left amongst many disused quarries to the outflow from Kentmere Reservoir, but the path to Nan Bield goes ahead.

A tributary beck is crossed in a pretty dell, and the path then climbs the east slope of the Tongue, the route being indicated by a line of cairns erected by Kendal schoolboys. At one point, where a quarry road branches to the right, is an upright stone slab bearing the inscription 'To Mardale': a relic of packhorse days. On the fellside to the right, across Ullstone Gill, is a disused quarry and below it a huge boulder, the Ull Stone, provides shelter for sheep.

When abreast of the top of the Tongue, the gradient eases and a splendid view unfolds of the mountains around the head of the valley, and Kentmere Reservoir comes into sight down below on the left. Nan Bield is seen a mile ahead as a lofty gap between Mardale Ill Bell, left, and Harter Fell, right; the path aims directly towards it and becomes a narrow track over open grassland. The ground steepens on the final rise to the pass, upward progress being helped by a series of zigzags, skilfully engineered not for the benefit of pedestrians but for the comfort of laden packhorses. At the top of the slope, the crest of Nan Bield is reached, adorned with a large wind shelter of stones, its back to the prevailing wind. A crude shelter that many a stormbound traveller has been glad to enter.

On a day of clear visibility the view northwards from Nan Bield is excellent. Mardale is seen ahead and below, and the long line of the Pennines closes the distant horizon. Retrospectively, the Kentmere valley is well displayed, the Tongue dwarfed to insignificance by the enclosing mountains.

The descent into Mardale commences at once, and after only a few paces Small Water and Haweswater come into sight far below: an arresting picture for the camera.

The path on the Mardale side of the pass, originally in the form of well-graded bends and twists to ease the descent, has unfortunately been cut to ribbons by the tread of impatient boots, the way down being a river of sliding stones where there is a need to walk circumspectly with regard to the placing of every step as the eye searches for firm footing; this is a bad case of erosion by careless walkers. The fine view ahead demands attention but should be observed only by halting; here the scenery should not be viewed while in motion or mishaps will occur.

At the foot of this unpleasant descent, the shores of Small Water are reached. This is one of the finest mountain tarns, deep-set in a wild surround of craggy heights, a gem of its kind, best appreciated when you are not in the company of others.

Small Water and Haweswater

Small Water

Below *Shelters by Small Water*

The path skirts the edge of the tarn, passing three stone shelters, these presumably being constructed long ago for the benefit of travellers overtaken by storm or darkness; they are still serviceable and can be entered by crawling, to the consternation of the resident spiders.

The path fords the outlet of the tarn and descends along a pony route by which early visitors were taken to Small Water. The issuing stream leaps alongside and, lower down in a hidden gorge, makes a final plunge at Dodderwick Force before proceeding quietly to enter Haweswater. The path crosses a declining moorland below the crags of Harter Fell and joins a track coming down from Gatescarth Pass for the last 100 yards to the road terminus and car park at Mardale Head.

A strong walker may return to Kentmere by way of Gatescarth Pass and Sadgill in Longsleddale. But not many will. For the weary, the temptation of a soft seat in a car and an effortless drive alongside Haweswater will be too great to resist. Nan Bield is enough for one day.

30 NEWLANDS HAUSE, 1096'
Newlands – Buttermere

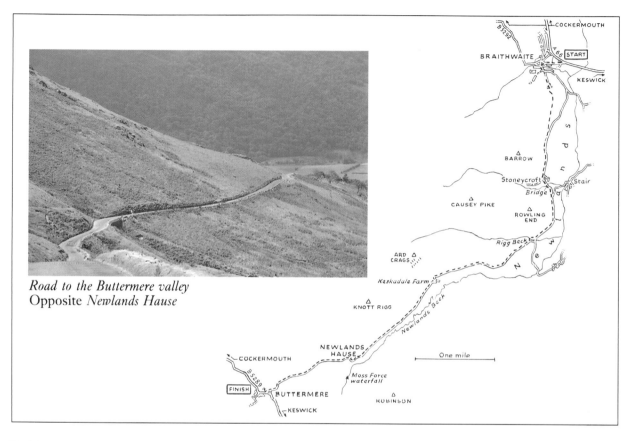

Road to the Buttermere valley
Opposite *Newlands Hause*

NEWLANDS HAUSE, often wrongly referred to as Buttermere Hause, carries a narrow motor road, non-commercial and normally quiet but much used by summer and weekend visitors to the district. The lovely valley of Newlands is patterned with country roads, any of which may be taken at the start of the journey. The most direct leaves the village of Braithwaite, then rounds the abrupt hill of Barrow which still bears the scars of disused lead mines, crosses Stonycroft Bridge over a stream where relics of mining activity can be seen in the form of a watercut, now dry, and passes along the base of Rowling End, elevated above the valley pastures. At Keskadale the road, fairly straight thus far, escapes from an impasse by steep curves to resume a direct ascending course to the hause rising along the flanks of Knott Rigg. Across the narrowing valley is the massive bulk of Robinson Fell. On the hause is ample space for parking cars from where Knott Rigg may be climbed or a waterfall, seen on the left, visited. Around the corner, the Buttermere valley comes into view with its attendant heights, a prospect full of promise; then the road starts a long decline to the village, allowing a more intimate appraisal of the delightful environs.

The road is not exclusively the preserve of motorists, and walkers can and often do use it but there is little opportunity to escape from the hard surface and at busy times it is best left to those who travel on wheels. Fortunately there is a direct alternative for walkers avoiding the hause, which is free from noise other than the tinkling of streams. This is the route alongside Rigg Beck (*see* page 151).

31 ORE GAP, 2575'
Eskdale – Borrowdale

THERE IS A splendid alternative route between Eskdale and Borrowdale, less spectacular than that over Esk Hause and having a considerable amount of rough and pathless walking, but because the way is guided by streams, there is little danger of going astray. This is a walk rarely undertaken, the adjoining mountains having the greater appeal, but in misty conditions when the tops are obscured it has merit as a foolproof route. However, it should not be underestimated; for most walkers it will prove a full day's expedition. Novice fellwalkers should not attempt the journey. In bad weather, it is safer to go from Boot to Wasdale Head by way of Burnmoor Tarn and thence over Sty Head to Borrowdale.

The route aims for the narrow col between Esk Pike and Bowfell, named Ore Gap and identifiable when reached by the red subsoil of a vein of hematite that gives the place its name which, occasionally and obviously wrongly, is spelt Ewer Gap.

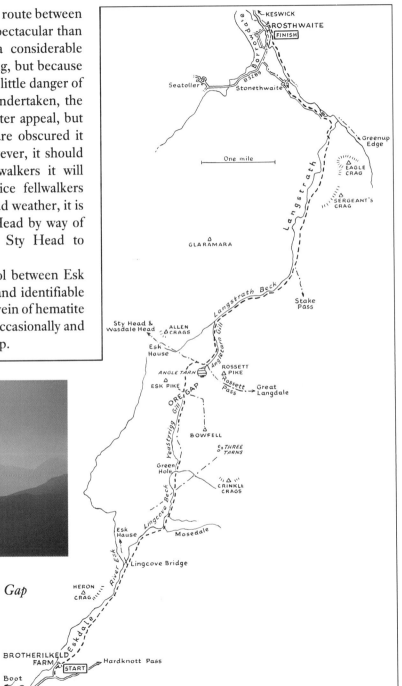

View up Esk Valley to Bowfell
Opposite *View to Eskdale from Ore Gap*

THE ESKDALE ROAD is left at the foot of Hardknott Pass, passing the farm of Brotherilkeld and continuing up the valley of the River Esk on a distinct path with an exciting mountain prospect ahead. The walking here is pleasant and the Esk a delightful companion, but after passing below the formidable cliff of Heron Crag, high on the left, the terrain becomes rougher as a confluence of waters is reached at the picturesque arch of Lingcove Bridge. Here the Esk changes direction, coming down a deep gorge on the left, the bridge spanning a tributary, Lingcove Beck. The way to Ore Gap does not cross the bridge, but proceeds on a path climbing alongside the beck, which here displays a series of waterfalls. Bowfell and Crinkle Crags rear up massively in front, and after passing the opening of another Mosedale on the right, in surroundings of wild and chaotic desolation, the path goes forward to a grassy basin on the left. This is Green Hole and here the hard work starts.

The valley of the River Esk

Yeastyrigg Gill   *Ore Gap looking up to Bowfell*

Abreast of Green Hole, the path thus far followed from Lingcove Bridge heads purposefully north-east, bound for the depression of Three Tarns between Bowfell and Crinkle Crags, but here is left in favour of a pathless crossing of Green Hole alongside the principal watercourse, Lingcove Beck. This stream emerges from a long and stony ravine, Yeastyrigg Gill, an uninviting chasm with the sole merit of pointing the way exactly to Ore Gap, not yet in view. The scramble up the bed of the stream is arduous, and better progress will be made on the adjoining slopes of Bowfell, which now appears as a massive pyramid of stones. At length, after an exhausting ascent, the ravine ends on an open fellside, the stream becomes a trickle, and Ore Gap is now clearly in sight ahead and reached with mute cheers. This is the end of uphill walking for the day.

Langstrath

A much-trodden path crosses Ore Gap, linking Bowfell and Esk Pike, and a distant view to the north opens up, revealing a kinder landscape with the promise of easier travel. Over the crest of the col, the way down starts immediately on a thin track aiming for Angle Tarn, seen as a dark circular pool in a green hollow below, and comes alongside it after a rough descent.

At the outlet of the tarn, the popular pedestrian highway coming over Rossett Pass and bound for Wasdale Head is met. The comfort of a well-trodden path is short-lived, the stream issuing from the tarn being followed down into the great hollow of Langstrath immediately in front and appearing verdant and restful after the arid wastes so far traversed. Ahead is a green and refreshing landscape, a valley set deep amongst enclosing fells: Allen Crags and Glaramara on the left and Rossett Pike on the right. The way down, on grass, does not have the advantage of a good path, but it is a pleasure to accompany the lively stream, here named Angletarn Gill and in maturity Langstrath Beck. Lower down a thin track forms and after two miles of walking from the tarn a distinct path is joined, this coming over Stake Pass from Great Langdale. Langstrath is now seen stretching far ahead, and tired feet will testify to the interpretation of its name as 'Long Valley'. But even tired feet will find the remainder of the walk a joy to tread.

Special delights of Langstrath are related to its charming beck, which flows along an alluring channel in a succession of bathing pools and cataracts and waterfalls. The enclosing heights, too, become more impressive, Sergeant's Crag and Eagle Crag rising very steeply to a rim of cliffs. Adding to the beauty of the lower reaches of the valley, trees appear in profusion and extend up fellsides which are coloured by heather and bracken.

Langstrath terminates at a delightful meeting of waters where a stream joins from Greenup Edge, the combined waters turning left into the Stonethwaite valley.

A bridge across the beck before the watersmeet and a path therefrom enters a rural lane that leads very pleasantly into the unspoilt hamlet of Stonethwaite, the cottages here being the first habitations seen since leaving Brotherilkeld.

This is a lovely corner of the district, typical of the romantic natural beauty of Lakeland and here still defended against modern intrusions.

A motor road connects with the nearby valley of Borrowdale at Rosthwaite. A pleasanter option, however, is to take the path alongside the beck for the final stage of the walk.

The Stonethwaite valley

Above *Langstrath Beck*

32 RIGG BECK, 1200′
Newlands – Buttermere

THE RIGG BECK route provides a direct way between Newlands and Buttermere exclusively for travellers on foot: it is not so much a pass as a deep cutting through mountainous terrain, rising gently to a low watershed from which streams descend on both sides. So confined and clearly defined is this crossing that only a genius could possibly go astray.

Opposite *The valley of Rigg Beck looking towards Newlands Valley*
Right *Ard Crags*

A GOOD PATH leaves the Newlands Hause road at the point where Rigg Beck comes down a pleasant valley from the west; there is limited parking for cars on the verges near the bridge. The path rounds a curve to enter a long straight furrow through the steepening fellsides of Ard Crags and Causey Pike. With Rigg Beck gurgling alongside, the path proceeds to its head waters; Ard Crags give place to Knott Rigg and Causey Pike is succeeded by Scar Crags, Sail and Eel Crags without any noticeable variation in the high skyline. These lofty enclosing walls effectively shut out distant views, but when the slight watershed is reached, the Buttermere Fells are seen in their full glory ahead. Past the divide, the role of guide is taken over by Sail Beck, the path following faithfully all the way down to the village of Buttermere in an environment of increasing beauty, being joined in its final stages by the path coming down from Whiteless Pike. Thus ends a walk greatly to be preferred to the hard road over Newlands Hause (*see* page 143).

33

ROSSETT PASS, 2000'
Great Langdale – Wasdale Head

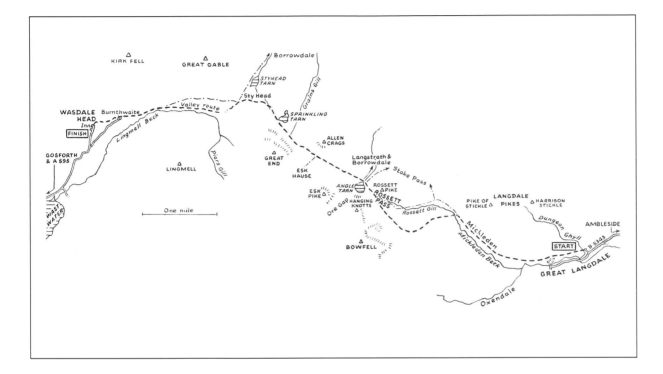

PASS WALKING has not the exhilaration and excitement of fellwalking, nor are the views as extensive as those seen from the ridges and summits. Lacking too is the interest of route planning and route findings: most passes have no easy variations from the well-trodden paths and there is no fear of going astray. For newcomers to the fells, walking the passes is a good apprenticeship for walking on the tops.

But there is one popular pass in Lakeland that comes near to the excellence of a high-level fell walk, one that affords intimate acquaintanceship with grand mountains, winds through contrasting and impressive landscapes, climbs to a considerable altitude and is exposed to the elements: in short, it deserves to rank as a first-class mountain expedition. This is the crossing between Great Langdale and Wasdale Head, generally and indeed almost always referred to as the Esk Hause route although this is a misnomer because the path does not reach or cross the true Esk Hause. It may perhaps be more accurate to refer to the route as Rossett Pass which is certainly crossed on the walk from Great Langdale although succeeded by higher ground before the descent to Wasdale Head commences. Two sections of the walk are uncomfortably rough and stony but can be avoided by grass alternatives mentioned in the chapter.

For full appreciation a whole day should be allowed for the journey.

Opposite *Rossett Pass*

BEYOND DUNGEON GHYLL, Great Langdale divides into two valleys, Oxendale and Mickleden. The path travels the two easy miles of Mickleden below the towering skyline of the Langdale Pikes, with the Band of Bowfell rising on the left. The valley terminates abruptly at the base of Rossett Pike, where a path branches right to climb to Stake Pass, the main path trending left and arriving at the foot of Rossett Gill. Nobody ever said a kind word about Rossett Gill. The direct climb is abominably rough, up a river of sliding stones through a height of a thousand feet; a torment of the flesh that only hardened masochists will enjoy. I had toiled up this ladder of loose stones dozens of times before discovering on an old map that there was formerly a pony track that made the ascent by a circuitous route across the lower slopes of Bowfell. I traced this old way on the ground without difficulty, finding it quiet, well graded and pleasant, and never again did I suffer the discomforts of the direct route. This alternative I recommend.

Langdale Pikes and Mickleden from Rossett Gill

It leaves the floor of Mickleden short of the head of the valley, fording the beck at a point I've never been able to identify exactly but no matter; the stream may be crossed at any convenient place and the pathless fellside beyond climbed half-right and across a landslide to a line of ancient cairns. The route thus far has been indistinct underfoot although, like many old tracks, plainly seen from a distance. Once found, with the help of the cairns, the path is a joy to follow, quite easy and within sight of the crowds struggling up Rossett Gill. It rises more steeply to a hollow threaded by many waterslides coming off Bowfell and crosses a causeway at a pool. Nearby is an old sheepfold, screened from sight of the valley below where, I was told by a Langdale historian, the dalesmen hid their sheep during the border raids. Within easy reach on a grassy mound, is a cross of stones laid on the ground, marking the grave of a packwoman who used to call at the Langdale farms carrying articles for sale and whose remains were found at this spot 200 years ago.

Angle Tarn

The pony route then heads directly to the top of Rossett Pass, appearing as a straight groove in its later sections, and here joining the direct climb up the gill. Some pony routes were devised for the pleasure of visitors and others, like this, were trade routes in the days of packhorses.

Rossett Pass, with grass succeeding stones, is a welcome relief to the feet, but a wild and inhospitable landscape meets the eyes. High on the left, the Hanging Knotts of Bowfell plunge into the waters of Angle Tarn; the tarn has been variously described as dark and sinister or as calm and lovely in its solitude. There is a short descent to the outlet of the tarn, and here you can see that the issuing stream crosses the path and descends into the valley of Langstrath, a vast hollow on the right leading down into Borrowdale. Indeed, beyond Rossett Pass, all the ground in sight is within the Borrowdale watershed, and the path over the so-called Esk Hause, straight ahead and much higher, is for some miles, until the descent of Wasdale Head from Sty Head, the catchment area of Borrowdale's rivers.

Esk Pike

From Angle Tarn the path goes ahead, climbing gradually to a wall shelter of stones, the highest point of the journey and commonly known as Esk Hause, although the true Esk Hause – i.e. the pass from Eskdale – is the higher ridge seen on the left between Esk Pike and Great End. The site of the shelter, at 2386ft, qualifies as a pass but only a minor one. The main watershed, at 2490ft, divides the gathering grounds of Eskdale and Borrowdale at Esk Hause proper and is not visited on this walk.

The journey becomes more exciting as the path leaves the shelter and descends gently, coming alongside Ruddy Gill where the vein of hematite seen at Ore Gap is again in evidence; this colourful ravine curves to the right, heading for Borrowdale via Grains Gill and a path accompanies it. The main path continues forward below the massive cliff of Great End, riven by gullies and dominating all else. Soon the shore of Sprinkling Tarn is reached: a lovely sheet of water that cries out for a halt; invariably rucksacks are cast off here for a rest while those walkers with cameras inevitably take the classic picture of Great End seen soaring above the indented shore.

Resuming the walk, the feature that compels attention is the immense pyramid of Great Gable directly ahead and increasing in stature as the path descends gradually towards it to arrive at Sty Head, a walkers' crossroads known to all who frequent the fells and from which tracks radiate in all directions. Away to the right is the inky pool of Styhead Tarn.

Great End from Sprinkling Tarn

Below *Great Gable*

From Sty Head, the path for Wasdale Head turns a corner on the left, a fine viewpoint and, with the promised land of Wasdale coming into sight as an inviting green oasis, makes a beeline for it. But over-use has turned the surface of the path into an uncomfortable channel of loose stones. Much better is the original path, now rarely used, known as the Valley Route, reached by descending at once from Sty Head into the grassy depths on the left to join the stream there: this, augmented by the flow from Piers Gill, becomes Lingmell Beck. The path follows it closely, arriving at the cultivated fields of Burnthwaite, from which a short lane leads to the inn at Wasdale Head and journey's end.

There are few, if any, grander cross-country walks than this. It will remain an evergreen memory.

Looking towards Newlands

Below *The summit of Sail Pass*

34

SAIL PASS, 2050'
Newlands – Buttermere

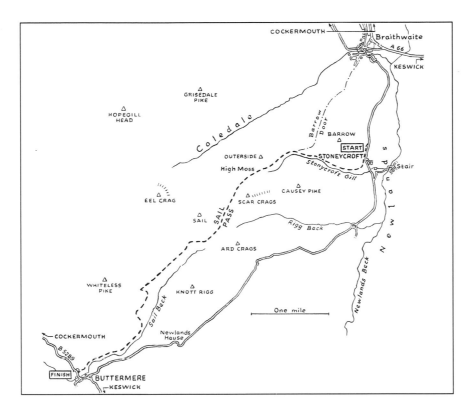

IN ADDITION TO the two crossings between Newlands and Buttermere by way of Newlands Hause (No.30) and Rigg Beck (No.32), there is another, rather more arduous, that takes advantage of an old mine road and gives much grander mountain views. This leads to a former cobalt mine of which a few traces remain, crosses a ridge beyond and descends to join the Rigg Beck route to reach Buttermere.

THE MAIN ROAD leaves Newlands at Stoneycroft, branching off at the valley road from Braithwaite, and soon starts to climb steadily up the side valley of the Stonycroft Gill overlooked by the imposing peak of Causey Pike and the heathery slopes of Barrow. It is joined after a mile by an alternative route from Braithwaite through Barrow Door, itself a pass, and becomes less distinct as it crosses the marshy plateau of High Moss before finally rising to the site of the old mine. There's a striking view hereabouts of the head of Coledale down below on the right and closely confined by the impending heights of Eel Crag, Hopegill Head and Grisedale Pike. Beyond the mine, the route, now reduced to a thin track, reaches a depression in the ridge above. This is Sail Pass, carrying a ridge path in popular use. Over the pass is the deep valley of Rigg Beck and a slender track, probably used by miners but little used today, slants down across the breast of Sail to the watershed of Rigg Beck and Sail Beck, the latter then being followed down on a good path to enter the village of Buttermere, arriving there in sylvan surroundings on a parallel course with the motor road over Newlands Hause.

35 SCANDALE PASS, 1680'
Ambleside – Patterdale

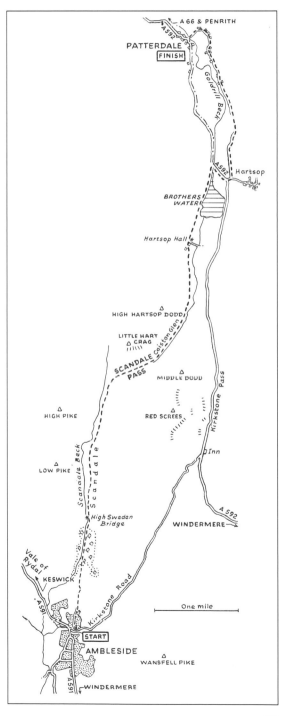

A CENSUS OF the travellers making the journey between Ambleside and Patterdale via (a) Kirkstone Pass and (b) Scandale Pass, would show the former route to be used almost exclusively and the latter, having no motor road, hardly at all. Even those who travel on foot seem to prefer the animation of Kirkstone to the loneliness of Scandale. Scenically, Kirkstone is the grander of the two by far, its untamed wildness being very impressive despite the tourist traffic it attracts. Scandale cannot compete in the matter of scenery, being tedious and dull by comparison, and its more limited appeal is due to its quietness and solitude.

AMBLESIDE IS LEFT by way of Sweden Bridge Lane, branching from the Kirkstone road near the old church. The lane climbs into an enviable suburbia, but when the residences and tarmac are left behind at a gate it becomes a rough cart-track. The next mile is perfect bliss, the rising lane affording exquisite views of the Vale of Rydal and the surrounding fells, while nearby Wansfell Pike assumes a stature that belies its rather modest altitude.

Opposite *The head of Scandale in summer*
Red Screes' summit rocks

High Sweden Bridge in Scandale

The lane enters a woodland glade and here is an avenue of loveliness, especially when dappled by sunlight; a musical accompaniment to the scene is provided by the rushing waters of Scandale Beck, hidden in a gorge down on the left. The lane is another of Ambleside's many treasures and is well patronised by visitors, their objective coming into sight at the end of the trees. Here is the picturesque High Sweden Bridge, a gem of its kind, its one simple arch spanning the stream. Everybody with a camera takes photographs at this romantic spot.

The bridge is the great attraction for the many people who walk the two miles from Ambleside, the prize they seek, and few aspire further along the valley to its head at Scandale Pass. This is not surprising; it must be conceded that the scenery beyond the bridge compares unfavourably with the beauty of the approach to it.

The higher reaches of Scandale are therefore likely to be of interest only to walkers bound for Patterdale. The cart-track continues upstream, not crossing the bridge, and rises gently, enclosed by walls, to reveal a different landscape, a barren wilderness where the many stone walls are the only signs of human intervention in the dreary scene. The track descends to a marshy amphitheatre hemmed in by the high ridge of Low Pike and High Pike on the left and flanked by the featureless slopes of Red Screes which reserves its interest for the savage Kirkstone face. Ahead is the pass, overtopped by the twin peaks of Little Hart Crag. The hollow is crossed and the ground rises steeply, trending to the right to gain the top of Scandale Pass, crossed by a sturdy stone wall.

The ascent of Red Screes may be made from the top of the pass, the wall serving as guide, but this side of the mountain exhibits nothing of the ruggedness displayed to the crowds at the Kirkstone Pass Inn.

The descent from the pass starts at once along the steeply declining valley of Caiston Glen, equally dreary and even more shut in by fells but having a vista of verdant greenery in front framed by the slopes of High Hartsop Dodd and Middle Dodd, the former terminating in a downfall of crags and scree where, in 1948, the efforts of the local dalesmen to rescue two trapped terriers won headlines in national newspapers for several days until the dogs were finally released.

With the high ground falling away sharply alongside, the surroundings become more open, trees making a welcome appearance, and then the path from Kirkstone Pass joins for the pleasant walk down the Patterdale Valley to the farm of Hartsop Hall, whence a lane continues the route along the shores of Brothers Water and to the A592. The village of Patterdale is two miles further or, if the road is busy, a parallel by-road from the Hartsop junction is to be preferred.

There is rural loveliness and quiet serenity at both ends of the Scandale Pass, but only drab desolation in its middle section. For walkers who choose not to be in close proximity to cars and enjoy solitude, this route is greatly to be preferred to the popular Kirkstone Pass with its endless traffic and noise. You will never see a buzzard or an eagle in the sky above Kirkstone; over Scandale you might.

The head of Scandale in winter

36 SCARTH GAP, 1400′
Buttermere – Ennerdale

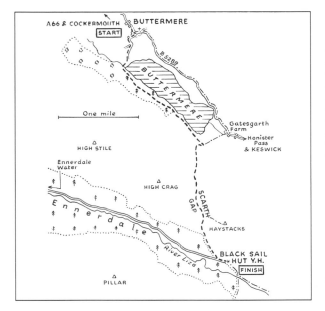

THERE IS NO WAY across the mountain barrier separating Buttermere and Ennerdale that does not call for serious fellwalking at a high level, and those who wish to travel from one valley to the other with minimum output of energy must have recourse to the Scarth Gap path which skirts the range to the east. This is a splendid walk, not long in distance but endowed with magnificent views; the camera is as essential as boots. Scarth Gap, often referred to as Scarf Gap in earlier days, is the depression between High Crag, one of the trinity of peaks forming the High Stile range, and Haystacks which is a lesser summit. The path is distinct, without deviations, and poses no problems of route finding.

Opposite The summit of Scarth Gap
Buttermere

FROM BUTTERMERE VILLAGE, either side of its lake may be followed, the more direct way being along the south-west shore, reached by a bridge over the outflow. Then amongst trees, some natural and some planted, the charming lakeside path leads for a mile below the majestic presence of High Stile, almost to the head of the lake where a cairned path branches off and climbs the open fellside.

This point may be reached more quickly by crossing the pastures from Gatesgarth Farm, this alternative saving a mile of walking but missing the delights of the lakeside.

The path rises steadily over grass slopes in the direction of Haystacks. Halts are justified by the excellence of the retrospective view over the Buttermere valley to Grasmoor. Scarth Gap is obvious in front, and the path leads unerringly to a large cairn marking the summit of the path.

There are signs at Scarth Gap that men have been at work recently trying to combat erosion caused by boots; in particular, steps have been made in the scree slope leading up to Haystacks. Early guide-books dismissed Haystacks as of little consequence and barely worth a mention, but in recent years it has deservedly become a popular objective of fellwalkers. I cannot agree, however, that steps should be provided to ease the ascent. Erosion of paths by over-use is a growing problem, but steps are not the answer. Steps up a mountain are incongruous, out of place. Steps are for going upstairs to bed, not for climbing mountains. Unfortunately, there are now many examples: there are flights of steps on Loughrigg and Nab Scar, and worst of all a stairway to the top of Mam Tor in Derbyshire – with hand rail provided. Heaven forbid, at least in Lakeland. No, the cure for erosion is for walkers to tread carefully and firmly on paths, not to kick them to bits.

A scene of grandeur greets the eyes on the descent into Ennerdale. Great Gable and Pillar rear up proudly across the gulf, Great Gable naked and unashamed, Pillar wearing an unbecoming skirt of foreign conifer plantations which have draped across the lower slopes for the last few decades. They reach all the way down Ennerdale and have no natural beauty. I saw Pillar before the trees came, in full stature, and it was a glorious sight. Now, its tears of lost pride and dignity swell the River Liza at its base. I weep with it. This should not have happened.

Gatesgarth Farm

Great Gable from Scarth Gap

The path from Scarth Gap goes stonily down to come alongside the dark cloak of a plantation, and reaches the cart-track now used as a forest road that follows the River Liza down-river for several miles to the scattered habitations near Ennerdale Water; there is a Youth Hostel midway. But at the point of arrival from Scarth Gap the only sign of civilisation is the solitary Black Sail Hut, most remote and isolated of Lakeland's Youth Hostels. Failing accommodation here, there is no alternative to the long trek down the valley with no respite from regimented avenues of battery-reared skeletons of trees. Where now is the beauty that was Ennerdale?

Pillar from Scarth Gap

The path to Skiddaw House   Below *Skiddaw Forest*

37 SKIDDAW FOREST, 1500'
Keswick – Orthwaite or Mosedale

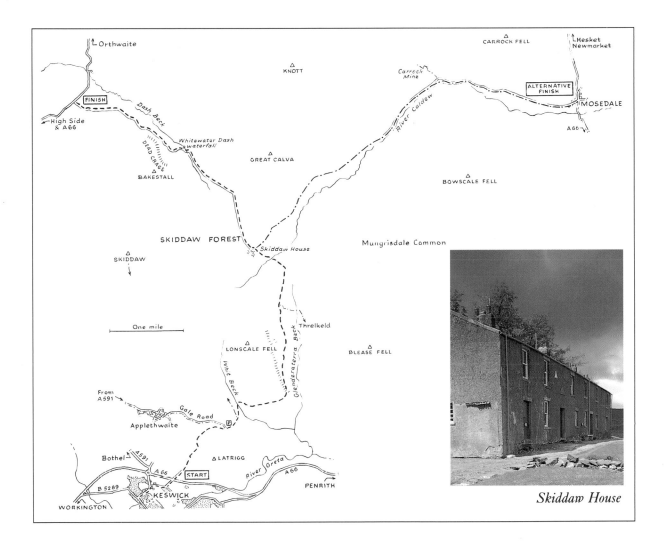

Skiddaw House

T HE NORTHERN fells of Lakeland rise in complete isolation from the Vale of Keswick and extend to the coastal plain of Cumbria as a huge natural barrier topping 3000 ft in altitude. This high mass, roughly circular in plan, is dissected by watercourses to form a score of separate summits. They are individually named and closely linked and nowhere permit easy passage between them except by two low crossings which divide the area into three segments, each having its own group of fells. These crossings are remarkably easy considering the high ground they penetrate, and are even negotiable by cars in parts. They start as one from the Vale of Keswick, branching in the heart of Skiddaw Forest; the main route goes on to the farming communities north-west of Skiddaw, the other follows the River Caldew east to Mosedale.

Dead Crags

STARTING FROM KESWICK, the small hill of Latrigg, 'Skiddaw's cub', must be rounded after crossing the new A66, either by way of Spooney Green Lane on foot, or by motor road via Applethwaite to the terminus of Gale Road; here the two routes converge and there is parking for cars. Here commences the time-honoured path to Skiddaw, heading north for the mountain. Around the first bend, the path to Skiddaw Forest branches to the right, makes a wide sweep to cross Whit Beck and contours along the lower slopes of Lonscale Fell, a terrace walk with lovely views of the Greta valley. The path turns north abruptly, in places cut out of the living rock, above the deep watercourse of Glenderaterra Beck, and now having the immense slopes of Blease Fell opposite. With Lonscale Fell displaying its rugged eastern face, culminating in a fine tower of rock, the path aims directly forward, passing an area of abandoned lead mines of which a few relics remain, and being joined by a path from Threlkeld. Walls come alongside, a gate is reached on a minor watershed, and the path trends left to the lonely buildings of Skiddaw House, built as a gamekeeper's lodge and later occupied by shepherds. A small plantation behind serves as a windbreak.

Here we are in Skiddaw Forest, a vast tract of open moorland extending into the far distance, a forest without trees, once a hunting ground and now a spacious pasture for sheep. Note that the sheepfolds hereabouts are circular, conforming to the Scottish pattern, and not rectangular as elsewhere in Lakeland. The forest is a wilderness, dreary under cloud, yet having a haunting beauty when sunlight dapples the landscape. The solitude is profound.

Skiddaw House is served by a rough access road, and if the objective is the pastoral countryside north-west of Skiddaw, this is followed below the shattered cliffs of Dead Crags into the valley of Dash Beck which has a spectacular but little-known waterfall called Whitewater Dash. Soon the fells are left behind and, amongst cultivated fields, a quiet motor road is reached between Orthwaite and High Side, the latter having a bus service.

The alternative route, for Mosedale: from Skiddaw House, the way slowly declines north-eastwards into the valley of the River Caldew; a thin track goes towards this pleasant watercourse and then comes alongside it. The track follows the river downstream on its north bank for three lonely but enjoyable miles as it develops bathing pools along its slaty bed. The track joins a tarred road below Carrock Mine, this leading into the hamlet of Mosedale along the base of the rugged declivities of Carrock Fell. From Mosedale a country road goes south for three miles to reach the A66 and its bus service.

Valley of the River Caldew

Above *Whitewater Dash*

38

STAKE PASS, 1576'
Great Langdale – Borrowdale

THE LAKE DISTRICT was not designed for motorists who, to pass from one valley to the next, must in many cases travel up to ten times further than the crow can fly because of intervening high ground. Walkers are better favoured although, even with greater mobility, they can rarely make crowlines or beelines and must seek the easiest contours. Nature obviously never intended Lakeland to be overrun by men on wheels, nor by timid pedestrians; it was fashioned as a rugged wilderness to be enjoyed only by lovers of solitude and primitive landscapes. One should be thankful for this.

Thus the two valleys most populated by modern tourists, Great Langdale and Borrowdale, have no linking road and cars must make a wide detour around Keswick to pass from one to the other. But walkers have one possible route that avoids rough climbing and reveals glories that motorists never see.

This is the Stake Pass.

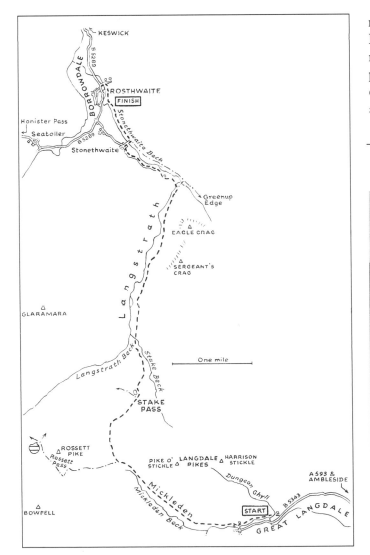

Opposite *Mickleden Stake Pass*

Langstrath

BEYOND DUNGEON GHYLL at the head of Great Langdale a much-used level path proceeds along the branching valley of Mickleden, set deep between the ramparts of the Langdale Pikes on one side and the rising shoulder of Bowfell on the other. After two miles of easy walking, Rossett Pike presents an insuperable impasse directly ahead and the path bifurcates, the main branch trending left to Rossett Pass and the other ascending grassy slopes on the right to the skyline depression formed by Stake Pass. The climb is unremitting and the original well-engineered zigzags have unfortunately been abused by impatient walkers who have yet to learn that a staggered path following the easiest slopes gives by far the most enjoyable mode of progression: thcsc untidy short cuts are invariably made, not in ascent but by clumsy walkers descending at speed, and are inexcusable. All mountain paths should be savoured slowly and treated with respect even in bad weather or when there's a bus to catch. They are the walker's greatest help in his wanderings amongst the fells and should be preserved with care, not kicked into unsightly ribbons of loose stones which can also cause accidents. I love zigzag paths and it pains me to see them wrecked unmercifully by walkers who do not appreciate their worth and do not deserve the privilege of freedom on the fells.

The ascent is dull, relieved only by the growing stature of Bowfell behind, but when the top of the pass is reached and crossed, a glorious prospect unfolds ahead as the environs of Borrowdale come into sight. On the right, the Langdale Pikes assume an unfamiliar outline, appearing insignificant over a wide moorland.

Gradually the path leads down into the long valley of Langstrath, promising a few miles of pleasant travel as a prelude to Borrowdale. And so it proves. Langstrath is lovely.

Down in the valley acquaintance is made with Langstrath Beck, an exuberant rushing of waters attractively endowed in its lower reaches with waterfalls and rocky pools. The path accompanies it along the valley, passing Gash Rock, a huge fallen boulder providing a few rock climbs. Across the beck rises the massive whaleback of Glaramara, and soaring above the pass are the unassailable heights of Sergeant's Crag and, further, Eagle Crag, both falling in scree slopes from dark towers of rock.

Langstrath has many temptations to linger over, but in due course a bridge spans the beck and admits to a lane in surroundings more akin to heaven than earth; rich carpeted fellside and woodland glades and the sparkling beck make the turn into the Stonethwaite valley a sylvan delight.

The unspoilt hamlet of Stonethwaite is reached with envy of those who live in this secluded community where little has changed since men first settled here and which still has an aura of seventeenth-century Lakeland. A tarred road shatters the illusion, reminding us that the days of horses and carts are over; this leads into the main valley road of Borrowdale, half a mile distant.

If Rosthwaite is the objective, a bridge over the beck can be crossed and a pleasant path followed to this hospitable village amongst trees and pastures; a most fitting finish to the walk that emphasises again that travelling on foot is so greatly preferable to motoring.

One is poetry, the other prose.

Gash Rock *Langstrath Beck*

39

STICKS PASS, 2420'
Stanah (Thirlmere) – Glenridding

ONLY ONCE HAVE I walked from one end of Sticks Pass to the other (once being enough), although perforce having to use sections of it on many occasions subsequently. It is almost sacrilege to describe any of Lakeland's paths as unattractive, but this high crossing of the Helvellyn range has little to commend it except as an exercise for the legs; it is tedious and drab and in places badly scarred by abandoned lead-mining activities. Sticks Pass is the only crossing between Thirlmere and Ullswater served by a continuous path, its one distinction being that it is the highest pass in the district in regular use. Formerly the highest part of the path was marked by a line of wooden posts, hence the name, but these have vanished.

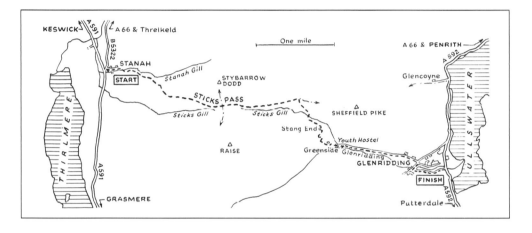

Opposite Looking up to the summit of Sticks Pass   *Looking west from Sticks Pass*

Stanah Gill
Stybarrow Dodd

STANAH IS A little group of buildings reached by a short lane from the A591 at the point where a road branches to St John's in the Vale. A path leaves here, crosses a small bridge, and climbs very steeply above the deep ravine of Stanah Gill, a gloomy chasm with many waterfalls.

The gradient eases when a sheepfold is reached, the cairned path then slanting across an open moor, the sprawling west slope of Stybarrow Dodd, to overlook the valley of Sticks Gill which is followed up to the source of the stream. Across it are the bare slopes of Raise which are normally unfrequented except when presenting animated scenes in snowy winters, being much favoured by skiers.

The final rise to the summit of the pass is steep. At the top the ascents of Stybarrow Dodd, left, and Raise, right, may be made.

The prospect ahead is not one to inspire enthusiasm. It is a scene without beauty, an arid and sterile landscape.

The path starts a long descent and is soon joined by another Sticks Gill. This is the only instance of streams descending from a watershed in opposite directions having the same name. At length a small reservoir constructed to serve the Glenridding lead mine is reached: this, having outlived its usefulness, has been abandoned and now appears as an unlovely muddy waste, and has been removed from the latest Ordnance maps. Beyond the bed of the old reservoir, a path goes forward and descends to Glencoyne but the main route, now faced by the slopes of Sheffield Pike, turns to the right and enters an area of industrial

devastation at Stang End where there are many traces of departed enterprise, notably a long flue that discharged at a chimney, now derelict, on the lower slopes of Raise.

With the Glenridding valley and Ullswater coming into sight, the path drops sharply in zigzags to the site of the Greenside lead mine, its scars grassed over and some of the buildings converted to other uses including a Youth Hostel. From here a road goes down to the lakeside village of Glenridding, its economy no longer based on mining but on catering for the many visitors to Ullswater. Here are hotels, guest houses, shops, a bus service and facilities for sailing on the lake.

Mining relics
The valley of Glenridding from Stang End

40 STILE END, 1100'
Kentmere – Longsleddale

IF, AS IS SUPPOSED, Garburn Pass was the first section of an old road across the south-eastern corner of Lakeland, its logical continuation from Kentmere must have been the cart-track into Longsleddale, referred to here in the absence of a name as the Stile End crossing. The way is distinct underfoot but happily sufficiently rough to break the springs of a car and is now classed as a bridleway.

Incredibly, an insensitive county council some years ago planned to transform this pleasant path into a modern road for the benefit of tourists but the scheme was quite rightly howled down by public outrage.

Kentmere village is left by the rising no-through road to Hallow Bank, this being departed from short of the hamlet where a signposted lane turns off to the right and climbs gently to Stile End; here two stone barns make a good foreground to the classic view of the head of Kentmere beyond. Through a gate, the track continues easily across open grassland to its highest point and then descends to Longsleddale ahead. In one steep section, the track has been badly eroded, an effective barrier to wheels, but is followed by a better surface as the track turns north below Sadgill Wood with a splendid view of the head of Longsleddale in front. It ends at Sadgill Bridge at the terminus of a motor road to the A6 and Kendal.

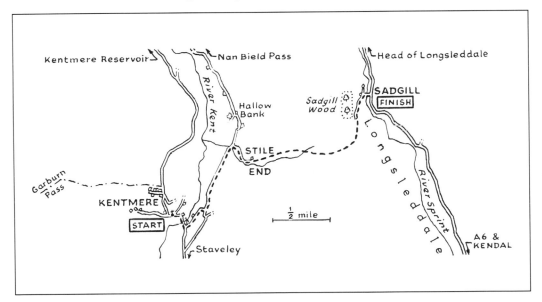

HAVING COME THUS far, which route would the old road take beyond Sadgill? Here it would be faced by an insuperable obstacle, high fells barring a straight continuation. The only feasible way for horse-drawn traffic was to ascend to the head of Longsleddale by cart-track (later used as the Wrengill Quarry road) thence heading across Mosedale and down Wet Sleddale to join the Great North Road (now the A6) at Shap.

This is amateur conjecture only.

Opposite *The head of Kentmere from Stile End*

41 THE STRAITS OF RIGGINDALE

WHEN IS A PASS not a pass? The essential requirement of a mountain pass is that it must permit access from either side, allowing a crossing from one valley to the next.

Seen from a distance, or on a map, the Straits of Riggindale would seem to qualify, appearing as a pronounced dip in a high skyline where the declining ridge of High Street falls briefly before rising sharply to Rampsgill Head; the name too (Straits = a narrow passage) promises a through route – but this is not so.

A footpath from Patterdale by way of Boardale Hause and Angle Tarn crosses an extensive area of foothills before rounding The Knott and slanting upwards to the Straits where it meets the Roman road traversing the ridge. Here one arrives at the brink of the yawning gulf of Riggindale, the way forward being abruptly stopped by a very steep downfall of rocks and scree with no possibility of continuing the line of approach by direct descent into Riggindale although this valley is soon to lead straight to Mardale. True, an adventurous walker may pick his way carefully down the crags and stone gullies but I write for ordinary mortals.

Riggindale is inexpressibly wild and has become a sanctuary for deer and fell ponies, foxes and golden eagles since the only habitation was demolished during the construction of the Haweswater Reservoir and the hamlet at its foot, Mardale Green, has vanished beneath the engulfing waters.

Prudent walkers arriving at the Straits of Riggindale and bound for Mardale complete the journey by going over Kidsty Pike and descending the easy slopes beyond. The Straits form only half a pass, and therefore are no pass at all.

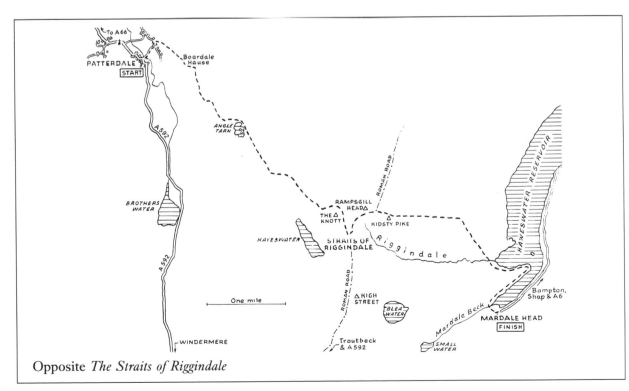

Opposite *The Straits of Riggindale*

42 STY HEAD, 1600'
Borrowdale – Wasdale Head

The top of Sty Head

SOONER OR LATER a very active walker in the Lake District arrives at Sty Head, usually on the crossing between Borrowdale and Wasdale, and most call here frequently during the course of their wanderings. It is a popular halt and there are few days in the year when walkers are absent from its well-trodden paths. The distance from one valley to the other is short, but the mountain barrier intervening is so impregnable that motorists wishing to make the journey must take a circuitous route of forty-five miles. This inconvenience led to an ill-fated proposal many years ago that a motor road be constructed over the pass; thankfully the proposal never got off the drawing board because of the weight of public opposition. Sty Head is a sanctuary of silence and peace amongst the grandest mountains in the country and should remain so. It is a place of outstanding scenic quality, staging a permanent exhibition of awesome impressiveness. This is a part of Lakeland that has never changed. Today's visitors see it as it has always been; to an old man it appears just as it was in the days of his youth, only the paths can show evidence of greater use and the cairns have grown in size.

Dalesmen have been familiar with the route for centuries, and there are signs that the steeper sections were originally skilfully graded and roughly metalled to ease the passage of laden horses.

'Sty Head' means 'The top of the ladder'. To many of us it also means Lakeland at its best.

Opposite *Sty Head and Great Gable*

Seathwaite   Below *Stockley Bridge*

THE WALK STARTS at the farmstead of Seathwaite at the terminus of the Borrowdale road where it is usual to find dozens of cars parked on the verges of the tarmac. Seathwaite is the wettest inhabited place in England, suffering an average annual rainfall of around 140 inches, and has been the scene of devastating floods; yet it offers a friendly welcome to the many visitors who pass through the farmyard all day long.

There is a choice of two routes. The original and usual path continues up the valley to Stockley Bridge, a picturesque stone arch above the rocky channel of Grains Gill. The path has been trodden to dust by endless processions of pedestrians most of whom, ill-shod and ill-equipped for rough walking, settle on the rocks by the bridge and go no further. Hardier souls bound for Sty Head cross the bridge and choose from a variety of tracks up the facing slope, which has been cut to shreds by the clumsy boots of those who see no virtue in following the well-engineered gradients of the original path and prefer short cuts. This section is a disgrace: verges have been trampled and vegetation stripped. Nature never gets a chance to heal the scars. On easier ground above, the path reverts to its old course by Styhead Gill, crossing it at a footbridge.

The alternative route from Seathwaite is quieter and more exciting. It was formerly little known and was late in appearing on Ordnance maps. This starts along a short lane from the farm buildings to a bridge across the Derwent, then following the river up the valley on the west bank through moist and rough pastures. The Derwent is formed by the meeting of Grains Gill and Styhead Gill, but before the confluence the path turns steeply up the fellside to enter the rocky confines of Taylorgill Force, a splendid waterfall. The path here is awkward in places as it hugs a wall of cliffs on the right before emerging into open country above the waterfall and continuing alongside Styhead Gill to join the usual and more frequented path at a footbridge.

A short distance further the shore of Styhead Tarn is reached.

Styhead Tarn

Above *Taylorgill Force*

Ahead is the massive dome of Great End and the giants of the Scafell range behind. On the left is Seathwaite Fell which, like the tarn, keeps its own rainfall records, and high on the right rise the vast slopes of Green Gable and Great Gable, split by the immense fissure of Aaron Slack. The wildness of the scene is accentuated rather than softened by the dark waters of Styhead Tarn.

The path proceeds to the highest point of the pass, a most important crossroads for walkers, furnished with a stretcher box for casualties.

From the large cairn, paths radiate in all directions. Here starts the popular Breast Route to the top of Great Gable, and a secondary and less obvious path contours to Kern Knotts and the Girdle Traverse of Gable. To the left goes the path to Esk Hause and Great Langdale, with the Corridor Route to the Scafells branching from it. The main path to Wasdale Head goes forward, turning a corner to face Lingmell's dark cliffs and the huge gash of Piers Gill.

Lingmell

Wasdale Head from Sty Head

The main path aims directly for Wasdale Head, slanting down across the flanks of Great Gable; through over-use it has become an uncomfortable channel of loose stones, appearing from afar as a great wound slashed by a giant knife across the mountainside. During the long descent, Wasdale Head comes into sight as a patchwork of small fields bordered by stone walls: a welcome green oasis enclosed by bare mountains.

An alternative way down from Sty Head is provided by the original path, known as the Valley Route, once long abandoned but recently restored to favour. This descends at once in the direction of Lingmell, easy grass slopes leading down to the stream flowing from Great End. A path accompanies this to the confluence with the waters of Piers Gill. High above is the long escarpment of Lingmell, and on the right Great Gable towers into the sky, seen foreshortened but imposing a majestic presence upon the landscape. The combined waters take the name of Lingmell Beck (on early Ordnance maps named as Cawfell Beck – a rare aberration) and a path continues alongside very pleasantly until it ends at a junction with the usual direct path. All that now remains is a stroll through cultivated fields to Burnthwaite Farm and a short lane to the little cluster of buildings at Wasdale Head.

There have been changes here since my early days. The primitive inn that was the Mecca of the pioneer rockclimbers has become a sophisticated hotel and cars have brought a new and growing clientele. Once all visitors wore heavy boots; today sightseers have introduced sandals. I liked it better as it was . . . But of course the mountain scene is unaffected by happenings in the valley and remains superb. Wasdale Head is wonderfully situated in a green hollow below an array of challenging peaks, Great Gable in particular rising starkly as a shapely pyramid. In this magnificent setting, minor irritations simply don't matter.

43

THREE TARNS, 2250'
Great Langdale – Eskdale

MOTORISTS WISHING TO travel between Great Langdale and Eskdale must make a roundabout and up and down journey over Wrynose and Hardknott Passes, but others unencumbered by wheels have available a splendid direct cross-country route with a single ascent and descent which, moreover, leads through impressive mountain scenery.

This is the Three Tarns route, taking advantage of a pronounced depression in the Crinkle Crags–Bowfell skyline, occupied by small tarns, usually considered to be three in number although there is a lesser fourth.

Coming up from Great Langdale, there is invariably the company of others engaged on the ascent of Bowfell, but beyond the tarns the way is unfrequented and rough underfoot as it threads a passage through a barren waste of rocks and stones undisturbed down the ages. The scene is primeval, but softens as Eskdale opens in front, waterfalls giving a foretaste of the manifold delights to come.

Opposite *The Links of Bowfell and Three Tarns*

Bowfell

FROM DUNGEON GHYLL at the head of Great Langdale, a level strath is crossed on a farm road to Stool End, and the steep buttress immediately beyond is climbed on a distinct path suffering from popularity. This is a shoulder of Bowfell known as The Band and the path rises steadily between the valleys of Mickleden and Oxendale. The ascent is tedious but relieved by fine views on either side – the Langdale Pikes arrayed above Mickleden and Pike o' Blisco overlooking Oxendale. The serrated top of Crinkle Crags, ahead to the left, demands increasing attention as height is gained.

Crinkle Crags from the Band
Below *The Band and Stool End*

Great Langdale

Below *One of the Three Tarns*

The path up The Band was formed for the ascent of Bowfell, and is the usual route to the summit of that noble mountain. When the ground steepens into the final rugged pyramid, it trends to the left to find an easy way to the top, arriving there ascending a stony and badly eroded breach in the rough ground above the depression occupied by the Three Tarns. The path is left when the tarns come into sight and an easy walk leads to them. From higher ground nearby, there is a retrospective view of Great Langdale.

The dominating feature of the Three Tarns depression is the extraordinary line of cliffs high on the side of Bowfell, deeply furrowed by a dozen steep and stony parallel gullies known as the Links and looking as though they were scratched out of the rocks by a giant comb; a formation unique in the district. I once descended one of these boulder-filled cracks and it was not a happy experience.

The tarns are unattractive, giving no cause to linger, and the route continues on a thin track south-west in the direction of Eskdale.

The track goes down along the base of the steeply rising buttresses of Crinkle Crags, its course amply cairned through a desert of loose stones and fallen boulders. When I first came along here, a very long time ago, there was little semblance of a path, the way being indicated by a series of very small cairns, simply one stone placed on another, and it was fun looking for the next. One stone balanced on another is all that is necessary in clear weather; too many Lakeland cairns have grown into immense piles, encouraging in mist or snow, but are today obsolete as paths have been trodden wider and more obvious during the growth of fellwalking since the last war. Too many cairns can be more misleading than too few especially when they have been erected off-route to mark a viewpoint or a dangerous cliff or a rockclimbers' track, all leading into difficult situations. But on the whole cairns are a great comfort when walkers are uncertain of their next move, and even the most experienced have often been glad to see one marking a path in bad weather conditions. During my early explorations in uncharted wastes, I was often mightily relieved to see a cairn that led me to a path. I love mountain cairns but not too many of them.

During the descent, a great rift appears in the side of Crinkle Crags: this is Rest Gill, offering a pathless and scrambling route direct to the top of the highest Crinkle; this is for adventurers only, while walkers bound for Eskdale continue down the stony track, reaching easier ground when Lingcove Beck comes alongside after crossing the grassy hollow of Green Hole. Looking back, Bowfell appears as a gigantic heap of stones, an untrodden wilderness. Bowfell's many attractions are all on the Langdale side.

Lingcove Beck and the path now go down into Eskdale side by side. Soon the cliffs of Crinkle Crags recede to give place to a wide grassy opening with a descending stream: this is another Mosedale, as dreary as the others of its kin but a pass in its own right, the crossing of its low watershed giving an easy route to Cockley Beck in the Duddon Valley.

Bowfell from Lingcove Beck

Mosedale

Lingcove Beck enlivens the continuing descent with waterfalls as the path comes down to the rustic arch of Lingcove Bridge and Eskdale is seen ahead.

Without crossing the bridge, the path goes down to greet the River Esk issuing from a spectacular gorge on the right, and then continues pleasantly along to the farmstead of Brotherilkeld and the Eskdale Valley road. The village of Boot, two miles further, may be reached by the road passing the Youth Hostel and the Woolpack Inn or, if these establishments are not of immediate interest, the village may be reached by a pleasant riverside path. Either way, the beauties of the valley will be seen and appreciated.

Eskdale with Lingcove Bridge

44 THRESHTHWAITE MOUTH, 1920'
Troutbeck – Patterdale

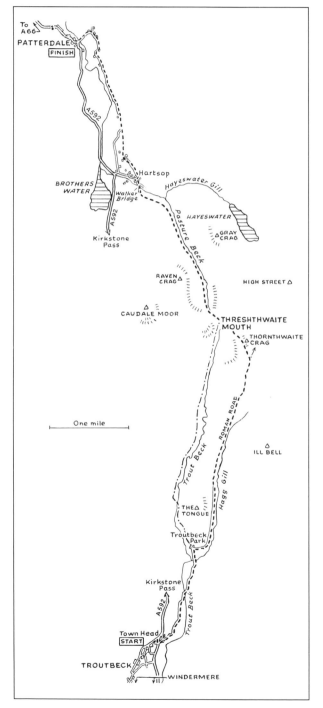

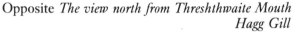

TRAVELLERS BETWEEN Troutbeck and Patterdale, whether on foot or on wheels, invariably make the journey by way of the popular A592 over the Kirkstone Pass. Walkers, however, can avoid the crowds of tourists and the hazards of the pathless tarmac by using a little-known route, roughly parallel, and proceed in blissful silence, out of sight and sound of traffic, over a pass in a wild setting between Caudale Moor and Thornthwaite Crag. This is a watershed named Threshthwaite Mouth and, although lacking the guidance of a distinct path, it is well defined by descending streams, and there need be no fear of straying.

Opposite *The view north from Threshthwaite Mouth*
Hagg Gill

THE A592 IS LEFT at Troutbeck village by a side road at Town Head that heads north along the valley floor amongst pleasant pastures and copses, and crosses the tree-fringed Trout Beck to reach its terminus at the remote farmstead of Troutbeck Park in a lovely situation at the foot of a wooded hill that appears to bar further progress. This hill is The Tongue and may be bypassed on either side, preferably on the right where a good track originated by the Romans goes upstream alongside Hagg Gill.

Hagg Gill is deeply enclosed; The Tongue rises steeply on the left and a lofty mountain range of which Ill Bell, scarred by old quarries, is the dominant height forms the skyline on the right.

At the head of this defile, the path most in use starts to rise in grassy grooves up the fellside on the right to the ridge high above. This is the line of the Roman road over High Street and is here known as Scot Rake, the reputed scene of a skirmish where the native Britons routed a band of Scottish invaders.

Troutbeck Park

Ullswater from Threshthwaite Mouth

Departing from the Roman road, the way to Threshthwaite Mouth goes forward alongside a wall until it turns away left as the declining slopes of The Tongue come down to eye level. Here the valley is again wide and the way ahead clear, although nothing better than a thin track need be expected on the final rise to the gap ahead over rough ground littered by boulders. Caudale Moor is a fine object half-left, rising in craggy tiers to a shapely summit; opposite is the steep downfall of Thornthwaite Crag, fans of scree dropping from a rim of cliffs overtopped by a tall obelisk. Trout Beck is rejoined, here in infancy, and in mist is useful as a sure pointer to the watershed at the head of the valley. This is Threshthwaite Mouth, crossed by a tumbled wall, and suddenly revealing an inspiring view to the north, a tangle of fells and a glimpse of Ullswater: a thrilling revelation.

The Tongue from Threshwaite Mouth
Raven Crag

Retrospectively, too, the view is pleasing, the Troutbeck valley being seen winding down to Windermere in the far distance and The Tongue dwarfed to insignificance by the greater heights around. It is always gratifying to look back aerially over a line of approach.

Threshthwaite Mouth is a lonely place, and in many visits I have yet to see another walker there.

The route continues over descending grassland towards a deep valley ahead and then drops more steeply to the formative waters of Pasture Beck which is followed downstream, a path forming on the left bank, along a narrow glen deeply enclosed by fellsides rimmed with crags. The path passes below the black precipice of Raven Crag, a haunt for rockclimbers, and across the beck slopes rise sharply to the long ridge of Grey Crag. A more friendly and open landscape with trees is entered as the pleasant environs of Low Hartsop are reached and the confines of the fell are left behind. Grass succeeds stones.

Pasture Beck from Walker Bridge

Below *Low Hartsop*

The path leaves Pasture Beck as it joins Hayeswater Gill in an area of former mining activity and goes on to cross the combined waters at Walker Bridge, an old one-arch span in a charming setting.

Low Hartsop is an old settlement and a few buildings preserve features that belong to the distant past. It is a living museum of seventeenth-century Lakeland. Regrettably it is now defaced by an incongruous modern car park alien to its surroundings. It is surely wrong to invite motorists to disturb this tranquil backwater; horses and carts would suit the environment better.

On tarmac again, the short lane through the hamlet joins the busy A592 coming down from the Kirkstone Pass and the illusion fades: we're back in the twentieth century. At the junction, a quiet by-road leads into Patterdale village two miles further and is greatly to be preferred to walking along the busy main road.

45 WALNA SCAR, 1990′
Coniston – Duddon Valley

FOR PEDESTRIANS, cyclists and horses the only easy passage between Coniston and the Duddon Valley is an ancient way that skirts the high mass of the Coniston Fells on their south side. This has long been known as the Walna Scar Road and in days gone by was maintained sufficiently to accommodate wheeled traffic, being much used for the conveyance of slate from the quarries alongsides. Both ends of the road are still accessible by vehicles. In its vicinity are identifiable remains of an early civilisation and, spanning the ages, this is where a local youth in 1954 took the first-ever photograph of a flying saucer (?).

It is a straightforward walk on a clear track made obvious by centuries of use, not in itself exciting but affording extensive panoramas of Coniston Water and the coastline of Morecambe Bay and over the watershed a glorious view over Duddon to the distant heights of the Scafell Range. The highlight, seen only by a short detour off-route, is provided by Dow Crag and Goat's Water, together forming one of the grandest scenes in the district.

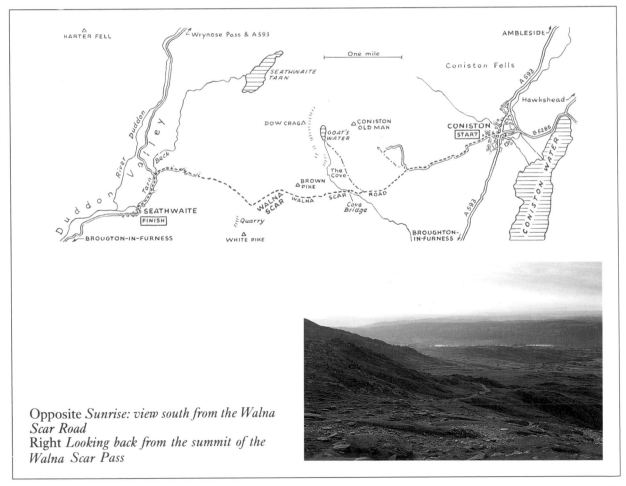

Opposite *Sunrise: view south from the Walna Scar Road*
Right *Looking back from the summit of the Walna Scar Pass*

CONISTON IS LEFT along a tarmac road rising sharply to the site of the former railway station which, in its heyday, was the terminus of a branch line from Foxfield Junction. This rural line, provided for the benefit of visitors approaching the district from the Furness area, and for commercial freight, was a casualty of the growth of motorised traffic, the passenger service being withdrawn in 1958. Above the buildings, the road climbs steeply, enclosed by walls and hedges, for a short mile further. At this point, a quarry road serving Coniston's main source of the handsome and durable slate that has won international renown, branches to the right and is commonly used for the ascent of Coniston Old Man. The Walna Scar track goes forward, having been improved in recent years since the reopening of another quarry ahead. Still rising, a small reedy pool, Boo Tarn, is passed and the reopened quarry is seen up the fell side on the right. Deprived now of its new surface but still very distinct, the track continues along the base of the Old Man with a wide moorland gradually declining on the left: this is the desolate terrain upon which important relics of the Bronze Age were discovered. After passing through a natural rock gateway, a branch path leaves on the right, this leading across a green hollow, The Cove, to a most impressive scene. The precipitous cliffs of Dow Crag are poised high above the bouldery shore of Goat's Water; if time permits, this short detour should be made.

Coniston Old Man   *Dow Crag from Goat's Water*

The Scafell range from Walna Scar

The main track continues, crossing the primitive Cove Bridge and then rising steadily with improving views of Coniston Water and the distant coastline. A small slate shelter with very limited accommodation is passed as the ground steepens on the final rise to the highest point of the walk, a watershed between Brown Pike on the right and the long level top of Walna Scar easily attained on the left. But, on a clear day, it is the superb view ahead that compels attention.

After the austere surroundings so far, the prospect from the top of the pass is as refreshing as springtime following a hard winter. Below is the valley of the River Duddon in a wealth of lovely woodlands and the green fields and scattered farmsteads of a contented husbandry. Standing sentinel above this realm of beauty is its guardian angel, Harter Fell, sprouting conifers instead of wings, and in the blue haze of distance, overtopping all, the Scafell range and the other heights of upper Eskdale.

The descent starts at once. The huge ramifications of the disused Walna Scar Quarry appear on the left and the track becomes a walled lane; it reaches the valley road a mile north of Seathwaite and its friendly inn. This last mile is delightful. Tarn Beck, a tributary of the River Duddon and often mistaken for it, races and dances alongside, embowered in trees. The main river in this part of the valley is hidden in a spectacular gorge.

The Duddon Valley is also known as Dunnerdale, this now appearing on Ordnance maps. It is a name I don't like and have never used. The Duddon Valley seems to me a sweeter name and more appropriate to this lovely environment.

46 WHINLATTER PASS, 1043'
Braithwaite – Lorton

WHINLATTER PASS has long been the recognised way from the Vale of Keswick to the Vale of Lorton and the Loweswater area, having had a road across it since early times. A century ago it was in commission by wagonettes on a popular sightseeing tour from Keswick, later becoming used for a bus service: today it is a fast highway for all forms of wheeled traffic. It is less accommodating to walkers who cannot conveniently escape the footpaths and must have recourse to the grass verges or forest roads wherever possible. It is an easy pass with few steep gradients and is sheltered by large plantations bordering the tarmac which unfortunately conceal nearby mountains from view. The plantations on the Braithwaite side are old, being indicated on maps 150 years ago; however they have been greatly extended and are continuous for many miles to the top of the pass and beyond.

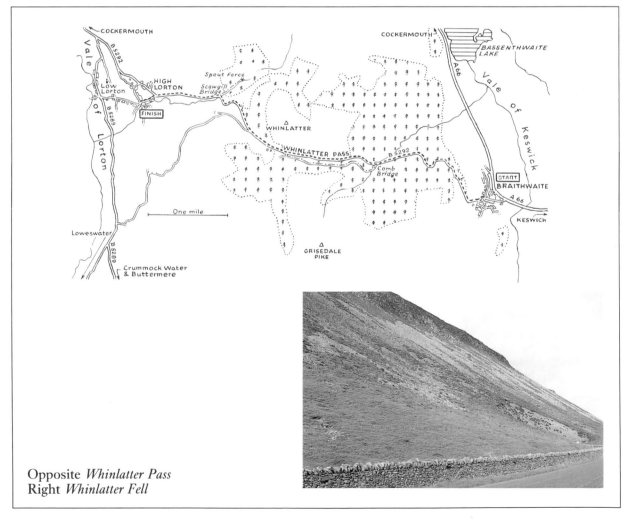

Opposite *Whinlatter Pass*
Right *Whinlatter Fell*

THE ROAD CLIMBS immediately out of Braithwaite, rising steadily with many curves, and soon becomes an avenue of trees which relent at one point to permit a lovely view of Bassenthwaite Lake and Skiddaw; this is a favourite halting place for both motorists and pedestrians.

Then follows a straight mile, passing a solitary building that was formerly an isolation hospital. Beyond, at Comb Bridge, walkers can pass into the silence of the trees on a forest road, from which branches another that runs parallel to the motor road and joins it beyond the highest part of the pass. Or the more adventurous may continue along the road from Comb Bridge and leave it to climb the heathery slopes of Whinlatter, which has escaped plantings. Walkers on this route first attain the ridge and then traverse this to the wind shelter on the summit, there enjoying a splendid view denied to those who pursue the road closely; Grisedale Pike, in particular, soars majestically from its skirt of conifers. It should be mentioned, however, that the direct descent to rejoin the road is both rough and steep.

Over the pass, there is a break in the plantations on the left and the lane branches away: this was the route adopted by the horse-drawn coaches on the Grand Tour in Victorian times. It is still, for walkers, the most direct way to the delights of Loweswater and Crummock.

The present road descends more steeply to Scawgill Bridge.

Bassenthwaite Lake

Scawgill Bridge   *Spout Force*

A halt should be made at Scawgill Bridge. Not long ago a peep over the parapet would have given a view of the diminutive bridge Scawgill replaced but this has now disappeared. Scawgill Bridge is the point of departure for a walk upstream to locate the handsome yet little-known waterfall of Spout Force. My first visit here entailed a desperate struggle through a new plantation, the forestry workers having completely disregarded the public footpath – a fault since remedied.

From the bridge, the road gradually descends to Lorton, a village in two parts, High and Low, which achieved a measure of fame when Wordsworth was moved to write a poem about a venerable yew he found there. Roads go south to Loweswater and Buttermere and north to Cockermouth through a lovely countryside that also deserves poems of praise.

High Lorton

47 WIND GAP, 2600'
Ennerdale – Wasdale Head

ALTHOUGH NOT CLASSED as a pass in guidebooks and not often used as such, the sharp col at the top of Windgap Cove between Pillar and Scoat Fell has all the characteristics of a true pass and indeed is one of the best defined in Lakeland. The ridge connecting the two mountains is short, a matter of yards only, and the crest is so narrow that ascent to it becomes descent from it in a few paces. The situation of the col is exceedingly grand; like an eyrie, the col overlooks a savage untamed landscape of crags and rivers of scree where solitude is absolute and silence unbroken. This is Wind Gap, attained from below only by rough and steep scrambling, and in terms of effort a poor alternative to the much easier Black Sail Pass. Wind Gap is for the adventurous and the lover of grim mountain scenery.

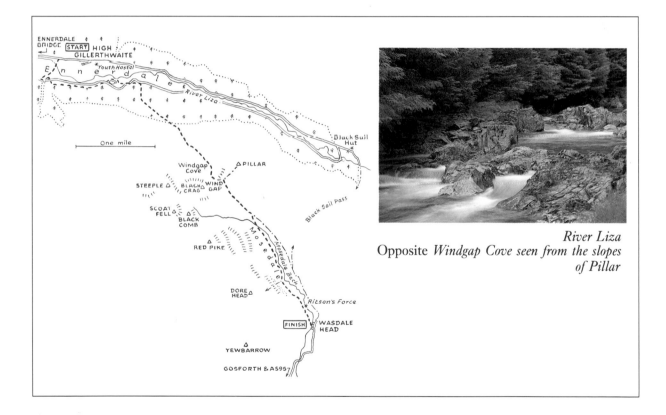

River Liza
Opposite *Windgap Cove seen from the slopes of Pillar*

APPROACHING FROM ENNERDALE, the first problem is to find a breach in the plantations to give access to the open fellside ahead, and this is provided as a footbridge over the River Liza near the Gillerthwaite Youth Hostel; this indicates a forest ride or firebreak that points the way to a stile in the upper enclosing fence. Clear of the trees, an exciting view of Windgap Cove is disclosed ahead.

Windgap Cove

Below *Steeple*

Pillar rises as a ridge on the left, Steeple is the tremendous declivity on the right, and the skyline directly in front is formed by the Black Crag of Scoat Fell. Wind Gap appears as the walk proceeds into the wild hollow of Windgap Cove littered with debris fallen from the heights around. The path is sketchy but the direction obvious as altitude is gained on steepening ground and, with Steeple becoming more imposing and intimidating with every step, the col is at length attained.

The summit of Pillar can quickly be reached from this point on a rough track rising on the left and it would be a pity to miss its extensive view at the cost of so little extra effort.

The path crossing the gap continues on the other side over the top of Black Crag to Scoat Fell. Ahead is a new landscape.

The valley seen far below and continuing towards the majestic mountains encircling Wasdale Head is the best known of the many Mosedales, and the path down into it is both steep and stony; much care should be taken. A long and tedious descent ends when the valley floor is reached and Mosedale Beck is alongside, its main flow issuing from the craggy recesses of Blackem (Back Comb) Head on the right. This is a natural sanctuary where few people ever go and the starry saxifrage grows profusely among the wet rocks and in moist crevices without fear of human disturbance.

Either side of the beck may be followed down the valley, the Ordnance Survey preferring the left bank and I the right, where a narrow trod leads below the beetling crags of Red Pike and passes a large split boulder known to the climbing fraternity as the Y Boulder; this provides a short climb that experts can accomplish feet first. The path improves when joined by the scree run from Dore Head, beyond which, with the beck now tree-fringed and deserving a deviation to Ritson's Force, it descends gradually through green fields along the base of Yewbarrow to the bridge and buildings of Wasdale Head.

Mosedale

48 WINDY GAP, 2450′
Sty Head – Ennerdale

WINDY GAP IS almost a twin, even in name, to Wind Gap, having the same features: a narrow col linking two mountains reached in ascent over very rough ground, and rarely used as a pass. It is, in fact, only of use as a pass for travellers coming from the east by Sprinkling Tarn and seeking a direct course for Ennerdale or Buttermere or vice versa in which case the long descent to Wasdale Head is avoided.

Like Wind Gap, it calls for arduous efforts and rewards those who do it with scenes of mountain grandeur.

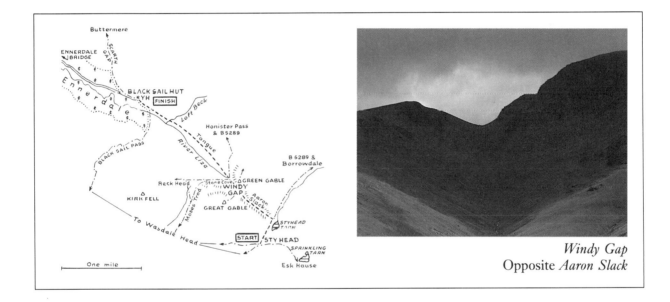

Windy Gap
Opposite *Aaron Slack*

THE FELLSIDE WEST of Styhead Tarn is cleft by a great ravine, given the name of Aaron Slack by pioneer adventurers who had a liking for biblical names. A track, often obscured by loose stones, goes up this defile, soon becoming deeply confined by the enclosing slopes that shut out all distant views. The effect is claustrophobic. Although not excessively steep, progress is slow and tedious, over tumbled stones and unremitting with no couches of greenery inviting halts. This strange cutting, between Great Gable and Green Gable, leads directly to Windy Gap.

After the arid and dusty recesses of Aaron Slack, arrival at Windy Gap is a relief; here too the awesome loneliness of the ascent is often dispelled by the sight and sound of walkers crossing the gap on a popular route to the summit of Great Gable. From this point, the top of Great Gable's summit is a tough proposition, its ascent and return to Windy Gap taking an hour, and longer if the superlative views from the top are to be studied at leisure. Apart from this tempting detour, the next stage of the journey, the descent into Ennerdale, can be prospected from the crest of Windy Gap, this valley being seen framed by Pillar and the High Stile range and identifiable by a dark covering of conifers.

Windy Gap

The descent starts unpromisingly amongst the boulders of Stone Cove without the help of a clear path, a way having to be threaded through a maze of rock debris, difficult to negotiate and needing care. Some recompense is provided as the cliffs of Green Gable come into sight, seen intimately at close range nearby. But the eyes turn quickly as the great arc of Gable Crag is fully revealed high above on the left, a formidable precipice split by intimidating gullies and cracks.

Green Gable crags   *Stone Cove*

Ennerdale from Windy Gap

The infant River Liza trickles from the desert of boulders in Stone Cove, soon becoming a defiant watercourse heading directly for Ennerdale and a perfect guide in mist. When welcome grass comes underfoot, the best stage to easy progress is provided on the right bank of the stream, where a thin track will be found on the long descending spur of Green Gable called the Tongue. This is crossed by Moses Trod on its way from Honister to Beck Head and Wasdale.

During the descent, the depression of Beck Head succeeds Gable Crag with Kirk Fell rising steeply from it. Beck Head also qualifies as a pass between Wasdale Head and Ennerdale, but few people will have used it as such since Moses made his regular journeys with his cargo of slate and whisky, the usual route from one valley to the other being the much easier and more direct crossing of Black Sail Pass.

At the foot of the Tongue, a tributary of the Liza, Loft Beck, is forded and a simple path continues forward to Black Sail Youth Hostel, passing a field of drumlins like giant molehills. At the hostel are the only beds for miles around; to find others in the valley a trip of several miles on forest roads is necessary – an anticlimax to the excitement of Windy Gap.

49 WRYNOSE PASS, 1270'
Little Langdale – Duddon Valley

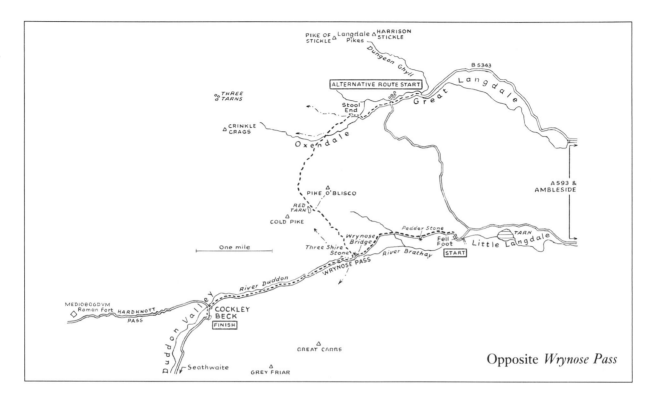

Opposite *Wrynose Pass*

WHEN THE ROMAN surveyors were planning a network of roads to link their forts in the north-west, they were faced with difficulties in finding easy passages for the movement of men and supplies in the mountainous terrain of Lakeland. Ease of passage, however, was secondary to directness of route; here, as elsewhere, a straight course from A to B was preferred. Their High Street is the best example of their fixation for directness, climbing to 2700 feet although simple but more circuitous routes were available. Another example is the road they made between their forts at Galava (Ambleside) and Glannaventa (Ravenglass). In this case, however, by placing a ruler on their maps they found that advantage could be taken of two passes through the mountain barrier. Little Langdale pointed the direction to a gap in the skyline beyond, now known as Wrynose Pass (Wrayene in twelfth-century records = path of the stallion); this was succeeded a few miles further by Hardknott Pass. From here it was an easy march to the west coast.

The Romans adopted this route and their primitive road can still be traced in parts although it is mostly overlaid by a modern surface: a narrow strip of tarmac winds unenclosed in a wild and untamed landscape and gives motorists the thrill of mountaineering without leaving their cars. During the last war, the road was requisitioned for military training and badly cut up by tanks and other heavy vehicles, but it was repaired and restored after the cessation of hostilities. It has remained narrow and unenclosed over the pass, calling for care and negotiation, in an atmosphere which, on a busy day, is charged with the expletives of frustrated motorists.

Fell Foot

THE CLIMB TO Wrynose Pass starts at Fell Foot, once an inn, at the head of Little Langdale; here the farm children used to man a gate giving access to the road beyond, but the gate and the children have long gone, as has so much of the Lakeland I knew fifty years ago. The road rises at once, giving a view of the Langdale Pikes and becoming unenclosed beyond the intake walls. A flat-topped boulder at the side of the long incline has the name of Pedder Stone, being a resting place for the pedlars who in olden days carried their wares in backpacks and found it a convenient height for taking the weight off their shoulders.

The road to Wrynose Pass

The stream coursing down the valley on the left is the Brathay, formerly a boundary between Westmorland and Lancashire. The incline halts briefly at Wrynose Bridge, crossing a tributary from Pike o' Blisco, and then continues at a steeper gradient with the Roman road in evidence alongside; it levels out towards the top.

On flat ground usually occupied by parked cars near the highest point of the pass stands a simple monolith, the Three Shire Stone, erected in 1816 to mark the meeting of three counties, Westmorland, Cumberland and Lancashire. All became Cumbria at midnight on 31 March 1974, and Lancashire lost its proud claim to own a part of the Lake District.

A path leaves here for Crinkle Crags and Pike o' Blisco and further, on the left, another path trends off for the ridge of Great Carrs and the Coniston fells.

Over the pass, the road descends sharply into the Duddon Valley below the steep slopes of Grey Friar, becoming level as the infant Duddon forms alongside on the two miles to Cockley Beck Bridge where Highland cattle may be seen grazing and the first habitation since Fell Foot is reached.

The road goes on down the valley but a branch crosses the bridge bound for Hardknott Pass. This is the way the Romans went.

The Duddon Valley   Above *The Three Shires Stone*

Wrynose Pass is not kind to pedestrians, who can only escape from the hard surface of the road and its traffic, in the absence of a footpath, by tramping along the rough verges. Nevertheless, it is a fine walk, best enjoyed in winter when all is quiet.

Walkers starting from Dungeon Ghyll in Great Langdale, however, can avoid much of the road and arrive at the summit of Wrynose by an alternative route along the Oxendale path from Stool End, climbing steeply out of this valley on a track that crosses a minor pass at Red Tarn and descends to the Three Shire Stone at the top of Wrynose Pass. This alternative route requires more effort than walking on the road but is infinitely to be preferred; the ascent to the tarn and its vicinity affords scenes of mountain splendour not seen from the road.

Red Tarn

INDEX

Bold type indicates the passes and their main entries; *italic* type indicate illustrations.